BRITAIN'S
SPORTING
MEMORIES

BRITAIN'S SPORTING MEMORIES

Unforgettable Moments from a Century of Sport

BANTAM PRESS

LONDON · TORONTO · SYDNEY · AUCKLAND · JOHANNESBURG

TRANSWORLD PUBLISHERS
61–63 Uxbridge Road, London W5 5SA
A Random House Group Company
www.transworldbooks.co.uk

First published in Great Britain
in 2012 by Bantam Press
an imprint of Transworld Publishers

© Transworld Publishers

A CIP catalogue record for this book
is available from the British Library.

ISBN 9780593070192

Addresses for Random House Group Ltd companies outside the UK
can be found at: www.randomhouse.co.uk
The Random House Group Ltd Reg. No. 954009

Writers: Giles Elliott and David Wilson
Project editor: Julian Flanders
Designer: Bobby Birchall, Bobby&Co

Typeset in ITC Stone Informal and Helvetica LT STD
Printed and bound in Italy by Graphicom

2 4 6 8 10 9 7 5 3 1

PICTURE CERDITS
All pictures © **Press Association Images** except the following: **Getty Images** pages 2,
5 (top left), 8–9, 14, 16, 55, 90 (bottom right), 99, 100, 105, 108, 116, 120 (right), 122, 124,
141, 146, 157 (left), 166, 184, 195, 213 and 214 (left); **Colorsport** pages 64, 119 and 154.

CONTENTS

Introduction by Desmond Lynam OBE

2012 IS A HUGE YEAR for British sport as we welcome the world's finest athletes to the UK for the Olympic Games. Landmark events such as these invariably rouse sentiments of nostalgia and prompt us to pause for a moment and dip into our own personal archive of memories.

A great sporting event affords us the opportunity to immerse ourselves in the collective excitement, the nail-biting anticipation and the sheer joy of witnessing the best sportspeople in the world all performing at their peak. There aren't many occasions that have the ability to unify, galvanise and excite and *Britain's Sporting Memories* is a delightful celebration of the power and the glory of sport.

My obsession with sport has its roots in a chilly, damp Saturday afternoon on the terraces of Brighton and Hove Albion's Goldstone Ground. Just ten years old, I basked in the atmosphere, captivated by the drama and delighted by the unmistakable thud of boot connecting with leather. I was hooked.

My fixation became my nine-to-five job and, thanks to a long career in sports broadcasting, I've been in the unique position of sitting ringside for some unbelievable sporting moments. Reading *Britain's Sporting Memories* brought a smile to my face – and at times caused me to raise an eyebrow – as I recalled some of the momentous events I've seen first-hand in the name of work.

There were the amazing Coe v. Ovett confrontations at the Moscow Olympics in 1980. The 1984 Olympic Games had their fair share of drama too, both good and bad. There was the on-track clash between barefoot

Zola Budd and America's sweetheart Mary Decker during the women's 3000 metres; there were the triumphs of the powerhouse Daley Thompson who shone in all his disciplines and went on to take the decathlon Olympic Gold as he had in 1980. Who could forget Gazza's tears in Italy in 1990, sparking the phenomenon of Gazzamania and bringing football to a whole new audience? Or how shockwaves reverberated around the rarefied atmosphere of SW19 as non-conformist Las Vegan Andre Agassi announced his presence on the grass courts in 1992 – and claimed the Men's Singles Trophy.

Britain's Sporting Memories remembers that, although sporting endeavour can bestow upon us great joy, it has also borne witness to some terrible tragedies. Though devastating, these misfortunes have not been without their legacies. There were the shootings at the 1972 Olympics in Munich. The untimely death of Ayrton Senna, the last driver to die in a Formula One race, led to improved safety measures in F1 racing. The victims of the devastation at Hillsborough are still mourned to this day but the tragedy saw long-lasting changes made to the game such as the introduction of safer all-seater stadiums.

Though *Britain's Sporting Memories* tells the tales we would hope to find in such a compendium, refreshingly, it also throws up a few surprises. The successes of our Paralympians are celebrated, as are the unique achievements of Arsenal Ladies Football Club who were the most successful football team of a generation. There are also entries dedicated to fans of sports not considered mainstream enough to be given much attention by the media, such as squash and badminton.

So I'm delighted to be able to invite you to sit back, put your feet up and plunge into this unique and entertaining treasure trove of triumph, joy – and of course, just a little bit of despair.

(Overleaf) Tickertape fills the air in Trafalgar Square as Londoners celebrate the news that their city has won the right to host the 2012 Olympics. In the twenty-first century this huge public space has been the scene of a number of sporting victory parades, including the 2003 Rugby World Cup and the 2005 Ashes Test series.

TITANIC
DISASTER

Part One
1900 | 1949

The Tragic Protest

Emily Wilding Davison lies on the Epsom turf (far left) with Anmer and jockey Herbert Jones. She died four days later in Epsom Cottage Hospital.

THOUSANDS OF Londoners had made the trip to Epsom to watch the Derby in early June 1913. It was a rare day out from the lowering city nearby and one of the most popular in the sporting calendar. The crowd behind the rail at Tattenham Corner (the sharp turn before the home straight, was particularly tightly packed) cheering the leading horses as they passed. Amidst the confusion, a woman ran out on to the course. Arms raised, screaming, she reached out for the bridle of an onrushing horse, Anmer, which belonged to King George V. The two collided. The woman was smashed to the ground, blood streaming from her mouth, an unfurled purple, white and green banner lying beside her. The horse somersaulted and landed on its jockey, Herbert Jones, causing serious injury.

For the next four days, until she died of her injuries without regaining consciousness, the newspapers were full of the story of the suffragette Emily Wilding Davison. Though her real intentions remain unclear, it seems most likely that she wanted to attach her banner to the horse's bridle and so bring the cause of women's suffrage to proper public notice. Although a committed suffragette who had already been to prison a number of times, Davison had clearly not intended to sacrifice herself that day as she had a return railway ticket and an invitation to an event that evening in her handbag. However, her tragic death ensured that of all the suffragette protests, it is hers that is most often remembered.

The 'White Horse' Final

IT IS impossible to say how many spectators witnessed the 1923 Bolton v. West Ham FA Cup final, the first at the British Empire Exhibition Stadium (or Wembley as it became known) – certainly more than the official 127,000 capacity. Estimates range up to 300,000 fans – enthused, perhaps, by the magnificent structure, completed only days before. One thing that is for certain is that the star of the day was not a player, but a grey horse called Billy and his rider PC George Scorey.

The crowd scaled walls, jumped railings and clambered over turnstiles. There was little the police could do to stem the flow. As the terraces swelled, then overflowed, the supporters poured on to the pitch. Enter Billy, appearing white in subsequent photographs, who, along with other mounted police, carefully eased the crowd back to the touchline.

Only minor injuries were sustained by a handful of supporters, one of whom fell foul of Bolton's first goal. A rocket from David Jack struck the unfortunate chap on the head as he leaned against the net, knocking him unconscious. The crowd continued to play a role, with claims they assisted Bolton in their conclusive second goal by kicking the ball to their winger, whose cross was volleyed in by John Smith – or was it? West Ham claimed the ball rebounded off the post, Bolton and the referee agreed that it came off another spectator behind the net. The goal stood. Questions were later raised in the Commons over the final ... on crowd control, not goalmouth technology.

PC George Scorey on his 'white' mount Billy helps to clear the huge crowd that had spilled on to the pitch before the match.

Wembley Wizards Run Riot

AS INSPIRATIONAL team talks go, captain Jimmy McMullan's 'pray for rain' on a cold March evening in 1928 ahead of his side's Home Internationals encounter with England leaves a little to be desired. Contemplating their team's line-up, the Scottish fans may well have thought that divine intervention was their only hope. Only three played north of the border, the heavyweights Davie Meiklejohn, Bob McPhail and Willie McStay having been dropped. The man set the task of suppressing the goalscoring phenomenon that was Dixie Dean had never won a cap – and Tom Bradshaw never would again, despite performing his role with considerable success.

Scottish prayers were answered. The rain pelted down on Wembley and the travelling fans realised their chances of success were greatly improved – the diminutive but fast and skilful Scottish forwards would make light of the heavy pitch. Despite an early scare when their post was rattled, the visitors were rarely in trouble. Three minutes gone and Alex Jackson scored with a header. By the 67th minute it was 4-0, thanks to another goal from Jackson and two from Alex James. Jackson completed his hat-trick in the 86th minute. A Robert Kelly free-kick gave England little consolation.

The Scots regarded the triumph as stylish invention over staid power but, for whatever reason, the SFA did not seem to regard this as sufficient. The Wembley Wizards became legendary, but never played again as a team.

Jimmy McMullan leads Scotland on to the Wembley pitch before giving England a lesson on how football should be played.

Golf's Greatest Year

IF IT HADN'T been for the Walker Cup, held at Sandwich in Kent in May 1930, Bobby Jones wouldn't have been able to afford to come to Britain to achieve the first two legs of his remarkable Grand Slam. At the time, the US Golf Association helped with expenses for team members when the tournament was hosted in the UK and Jones took advantage of this for his last opportunity to win all four Majors in a season – back then the US and British Opens and the US and British Amateur Opens – before concentrating on his law career. For Jones, the greatest obstacle was the British Amateur, held at the St Andrews links. Jones had won the US Open and US Amateur Open four times each, and the British Open twice, but had failed in his two attempts at the British Amateur title.

Bobby Jones is escorted through the crowds and back to the clubhouse after winning the British Amateur at St Andrews.

Once again it was almost his undoing. In the match play tournament, Jones won his fourth-round tie against Englishman Cyril Tolley, the reigning champion, at the first extra hole. In the following round, he found himself 2 down with 5 to play, his poor form blamed on a glass of sherry at lunch, but he snatched victory on the 18th green. The 36-hole final itself proved more straightforward, a comfortable 7 & 6 win over Roger Wethered. Over the following weeks, legs two, three and four fell with relative ease. To be the first to claim one of sport's landmark achievements is a mark of greatness; 80 years later to still be the only one is something else altogether.

Tragedy at Ibrox

'THEY NEVER DIE who live in the hearts they leave behind.' These words appear on the gravestone of John Thomson, Celtic's athletic, courageous and hugely talented Scottish international goalkeeper who died at the age of 22 following a terrible accident playing the game at which he excelled.

The year before his death, Thomson, from Cardenden in Fife, suffered dreadful injuries during a match against Airdrie. When his brother Jim told him that he would have to change his style of play or something even worse could happen, Thomson replied, 'The only thing I see is the ball and it has to be mine.'

Exactly 19 months later, minutes into the second half of the Old Firm game at Ibrox, Rangers striker Sam English ran on to a through ball played into the Celtic box. Thomson charged from his line and dived. English was blameless for the collision that occurred, but as the ball drifted past the post, Thomson lay still. He was stretchered off the pitch and died later that evening as a result of a depressed fracture of the skull. Thomson's fiancée was in the crowd that day at Ibrox.

Such was the impact on the football community in Scotland that 40,000 people turned up at Thomson's funeral four days later. He is keenly remembered to this day.

Celtic keeper John Thomson dives bravely at the feet of Rangers' Sam English – it was the final save of his fledgling career.

The Bodyline Controversy

UNSPORTSMANLIKE BEHAVIOUR. It has always been difficult to define; for every person, or nation, there's a different line of acceptability beyond which you cannot tread in order to win. Cricket, despite its gentlemanly image, has always had its problems with dastardly deeds. Australia are often at the centre of them. Most famously, underhand tactics were used against them in the Bodyline Ashes.

It was only in the Third Test in Adelaide in January 1933, with the series nicely poised at 1-1, that the controversy really erupted. You would hardly have known it from the demeanour of the opposing captains Douglas Jardine and Bill Woodfull at the toss. But when deliveries from Harold Larwood thumped first into Woodfull's chest and then Bert Oldfield's head, the cricket world was at war.

Neither delivery was strictly bodyline, with its tactic of overloading the leg side with fielders and bowling at the man, but Jardine had authorised any ball that unsettled the Australian batsmen, specifically Don Bradman. In fact, Gubby Allen, who refused to bowl bodyline, took more wickets than Larwood in Adelaide; but the Nottinghamshire quickie had The Don's number. He removed his man four times in six innings, and England, superior in every department, regained the Ashes. Fair dinkum?

Captains Douglas Jardine (left) and Bill Woodfull toss up before the 'cricket war' that began at the Adelaide Oval in January 1933.

TENNIS All England Lawn Tennis Championships
Men's Singles Final, Fred Perry v. Gottfried von Cramm, Wimbledon, London, 14 July 1936

1936

The Last British Man to Win Wimbledon

AS IT IS rarely mentioned, especially in the Henman and Murray households, it is worth noting that with his 1936 victory, Fred Perry became the last British winner of the Wimbledon men's singles title. Facing Perry, for the second year running, was German Baron Gottfried von Cramm, and if you had dallied too long over your strawberries and cream, you could easily have missed the entire match.

Perry took a mere 40 minutes to demolish the Baron and secure his third consecutive title. It was the second shortest men's final of all time, with WC Renshaw's defeat of JT Hartley in 1881 beating it by three minutes. Not to be outdone, Perry's win holds the record for the fewest games played in a final, 6-1, 6-1, 6-0. It could be conjectured that Perry didn't enjoy playing in Wimbledon's showpiece, and he certainly didn't hang around. The total duration of his three finals is 192 minutes and, even given that there were no breaks between changeovers, this is an extraordinary achievement.

Not that the crowds minded his abbreviated appearances. Perry's Stockport upbringing may have set him apart from the elite class that dominated the All England Club, but the fans loved him, his play and his good looks. Fred Perry will always hold the most special place in the hearts of British tennis enthusiasts and, should a British man win the title, it is a sure bet that before long Perry will be referred to as 'the last British winner of all four Grand Slams'.

Speed and athleticism were Fred Perry's main weapons; both were on show as he crushed Baron Gottfried von Cramm to win his third Wimbledon men's singles title in a row.

Prince Obolensky's Match

Prince Obolensky (left) – scorer of one of English rugby's most famous tries.

HAS THERE ever been a more exotic 'English' rugby player or a more glorious international debut?

The short answer is no. The infant Prince Alexander Obolensky, born in Petrograd, the son of an officer of Tsar Nicholas II's Imperial Guard, escaped Russia with his family following the 1917 Revolution and settled in London. He was educated in Derbyshire and later went to Oxford University, where he excelled at sport, earning two rugby Blues. He was rather less successful at studying, eventually receiving a fourth class degree.

Not that it mattered. With his style and charisma, the prince was destined for greatness. His call-up to the England team for the 1936 match against the All Blacks caused some controversy as it was unclear whether he had officially been granted British citizenship.

Afterwards, such issues were trivial irrelevancies. England had lost both their previous encounters with New Zealand, but Obolensky put paid to that record with two blistering first-half tries built on pace and balance, sidesteps and swerve. Six points to the prince, to which the tourists had no response, eventually succumbing 13-0.

Incredibly, Obolensky won only three more caps for England, but on 29 March 1940 he was again named in the squad for a game against Wales. The following day, while training with the RAF, for whom he had volunteered, his Hawker Hurricane caught its wheels in a rabbit warren after landing. The plane dropped into a ravine at the end of the runway, an accident in which the young pilot officer broke his neck. He was 24 years old.

The Don Bows Out with a Duck

Bradman faces the press at Worcester before the first match of his final international tour in April 1948.

THE GREATEST batsman of all time walked out for the fifth and final Test of the 1948 Ashes series with Australia on 117 for 1 in reply to England's first innings total of 52 all out. Australia were 3–0 up in the series. Australian captain Don Bradman was playing in the final Test (his 52nd) of his incredible career. In 51 Tests and 79 innings, Bradman had scored 6,996 runs at an average of 101.39. No one then, or since, has come anywhere near that figure. As he walked towards the wicket, the crowd of 30,000 gave him a standing ovation, the England players clapped him and captain Norman Yardley called for three cheers. Bradman needed four more runs to end his career with an average of a century or more. With order resumed, he prepared to face spin bowler Eric Hollies. The first ball was gently pushed away. John Arlott of the BBC described the second ball, a googly, 'Hollies pitches the ball up slowly and ... he's bowled! [Silence] Bradman bowled Hollies 0 ... What do you say under those circumstances?' Apparently, what Bradman said back in the pavilion was, 'Gee whiz, funny doing that.' With Australia winning by an innings and 149 runs, he did not have another chance to bat. He is still the greatest batsman of all time and 99.94 is still a barely believable average. And sport once again reminded us that no player is bigger than the game itself. That's a good thing.

London Hosts Austerity Olympics

OLYMPIC SCANDAL and outrage is nothing new. In 1936 Hitler attempted to turn the Berlin Olympiad into a Nazi propaganda event and a demonstration of racial superiority. The 1940 event was due to take place in Japan, despite widespread condemnation of the invasion of China in 1937. Then the Second World War broke out and everything was put on hold.

Before the conflict began, London had been announced as the 1944 host and when the Olympic Committee met to decide on the venue for the first post-war Games, Britain's capital was the obvious choice. The Games were promoted as a celebration of peace. The country was still a long way from recovery and in retrospect the Games have became known as the Austerity Games because of the straitened circumstances in which they were held. Ironically, many believe they were the last Games that truly represented the spirit

of competition and cooperation on which the Olympic movement is based.

No new stadiums were built – there was a shortage of manual labour and finance. Competing countries sent building materials to help with renovations. There was no Olympic Village – housing was scarce. Competitors stayed in RAF campsites and schools. Rationing was in force – nations supplied fruit, vegetables, eggs and food parcels. Athletes were transported in double-decker buses. A record 59 countries participated (Germany and Japan were not invited, the Soviet Union declined) and the sun shone on the opening ceremony. The Games were a huge success. Wonderful athletes such as the Dutch runner Fanny Blankers-Koen – known as the Flying Housewife – mesmerised the crowds and the spirit of the Olympics was rekindled following the dark days of war.

Fanny Blankers-Koen on her way to a new world record in the 80 metres hurdles.

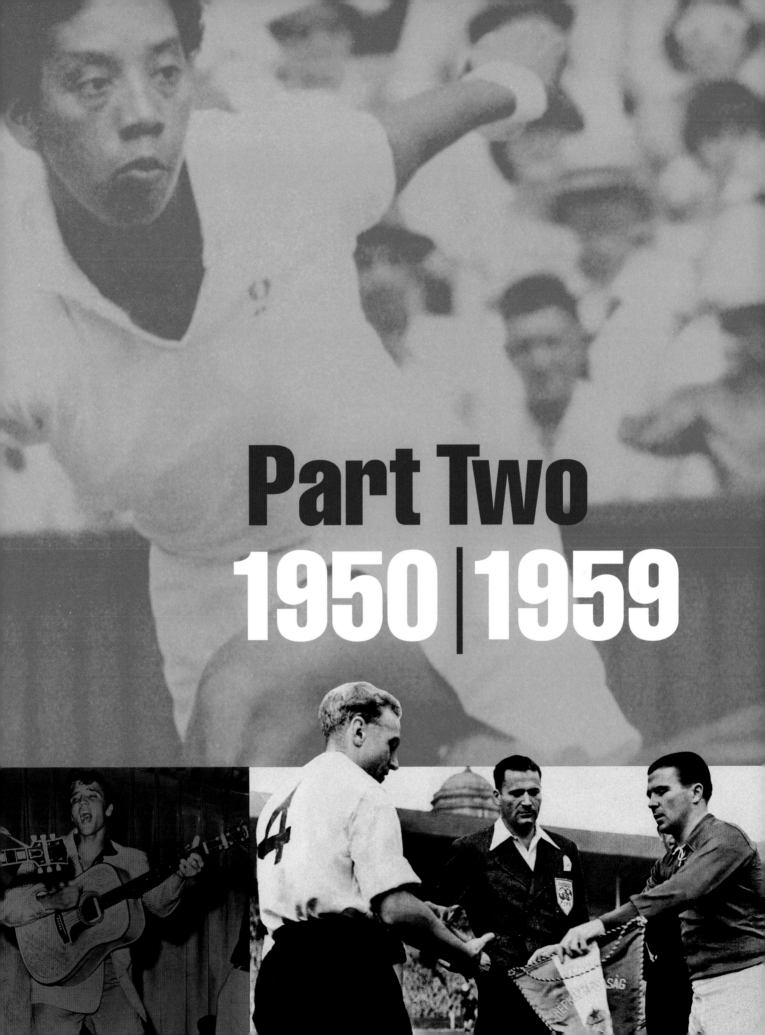

Part Two
1950 | 1959

England Humiliated by USA

USA supporters chair their goalscoring centre forward Joe Gaetjens from the pitch after England's astonishing defeat.

JOE GAETJENS may not be a name that immediately comes to mind when listing legendary strikers, but his 37th-minute diving header led to one of the greatest upsets in international football. Needless to say, they made a film about it. In the USA, their 1-0 victory over England in the 1950 World Cup is known as 'The Miracle on Grass'. We don't have a printable name for it.

This was England's first venture into a tournament treated with suspicion by the FA, to the extent that they sent a second team of internationals, including Stanley Matthews, on a tour of Canada at the same time. Matthews later joined the World Cup squad, but did not play in the USA game. Even so, a strong England side featured Alf Ramsey, Billy Wright, Wilf Mannion, Tom Finney and Stan Mortensen. The USA team had one full-time professional and included a postman and an undertaker. Haitian-born Gaetjens, who never became a US citizen and is reported to have died in mysterious circumstances in Haiti in 1964, was a student and sometime dishwasher.

England, devastated, crashed out of the competition in the next match, losing to Spain. While Gaetjens took the plaudits, perhaps the real US hero was goalkeeper Frank Borghi, who made a succession of crucial saves. In the movie, he was played by Scottish actor Gerard Butler; it was a role he probably rather enjoyed.

Britain's First Black World Boxing Champion

RANDOLPH TURPIN, the 23-year-old from Leamington Spa, taking on the boxing god that was Sugar Ray Robinson for the World Middleweight Championship. Surely the result was a foregone conclusion? The boxing press and the bookies thought so. Robinson was too good, too experienced and too flashy. He arrived in the UK with a fuchsia-coloured Cadillac for goodness sake.

But the British and European titleholder was no stranger to sideshow distractions, having boxed in fairground booths. Although lacking experience (Turpin's professional record of 46 fights with two losses compared to Robinson's 133 with one defeat), he had trained and was strong and fit. Robinson had arrived in England after a series of non-title fights across Europe and had not focused on the encounter with the same intensity as Turpin.

An accidental clash of heads in the seventh round left Robinson more damaged than the challenger. By the 15th and final round, the crowd were singing 'For he's a jolly good fellow' and when the final bell rang, Robinson had no complaints as the referee raised Turpin's hand.

It was a sensational victory – Turpin was Britain's first world boxing champion since 1891. Sixty-four days later, he lost the rematch in New York, which now looks like the first step in a tragic decline. In 1966, Turpin shot and killed himself.

Randolph Turpin (left) unleashes an explosive left, narrowly missing Sugar Ray Robinson's ear.

TENNIS All England Lawn Tennis Championships
Ladies' Singles Final, Maureen Connolly v. Louise Brough, Wimbledon, London, 5 July 1952

1952

Little Mo: She Came, She Saw, She Won

'LITTLE MO' – as a moniker it sounds so quaint, cutesy even. And on one level it was spot-on for Maureen Connolly – a California-born, polite, outgoing, 5-foot 4-inch 17-year-old with an all-American smile. But at the sporting level, her nickname masked a ruthless, strong, fast, dynamic athlete with an armoury of strokes unparalleled in the game at the time.

She arrived in SW19 in 1952 as the youngest ever winner of the US Championship (now the US Open) and left with the first of her three ladies' singles titles, having beaten compatriot Louise Brough Clapp 6-4, 6-3. Over the course of that unbeaten run, she lost only two sets. The statistics of Mo's career almost defy belief. From her victory in the 1951 US Championships, at the age of 16, she won the following eight Grand Slam events she entered, and in 1953 she became the first woman and only the second person ever to win the Grand Slam of all four major tournaments in a year, losing just one set in the process.

Then, in July 1954, on the back of her third Wimbledon triumph, she suffered a horse-riding accident and retired from the game, aged just nineteen. Fifteen years later, cancer took her for ever. For all too short a time, Little Mo lit the world of tennis with a brilliant flame.

Mighty 'Little Mo' Connolly had the skill and determination to give her an unbeaten singles record at Wimbledon.

Matthews Gets His Medal

It's poetry in motion as Stanley Matthews puts in the perfect cross for Blackpool's left winger Bill Perry to score his side's cup-winning fourth goal.

MANY PEOPLE regarded the 1953 FA Cup final between Blackpool and Bolton as Stanley Matthews' last chance at silverware. He was 38 after all. He had mesmerised fans, confounded defenders and graced football for over twenty years, with no winners' medals to show for it. Having lost with Blackpool in the 1948 and 1951 finals, everyone, bar Bolton fans, was rooting for him this time round.

Within two minutes, however, the dream was in trouble, when Nat Lofthouse's 25-yard shot went straight through the Seasiders' keeper George Farm and into the net. Blackpool drew level after 35 minutes when Stan Mortensen's shot was deflected in. Less than five minutes later, Bolton were back in front and after 55 minutes it was 3-1, but an injury to Bolton centre-half, Eric Bell, offered a chink of light to Blackpool, and

Matthews in particular. He began to turn on the style and torment the Bolton defence.

With 22 minutes remaining, Matthews crossed, the keeper fumbled the ball and Mortensen stabbed it home – 3-2. With just three minutes to go, Mortensen completed his hat-trick with a free-kick – 3-3. In the dying seconds, Matthews once again found space and cut the ball back for Bill Perry to shoot home from 10 yards. To a rapturous reception, Matthews was carried off the pitch on his teammates' shoulders, with the TV commentator noting, 'What an end to a great career.' Four years later, Matthews was still playing for England.

'Knight' Wins the Derby – at Last

SIR GORDON RICHARDS' career statistics are astonishing. In 1933 he rode 12 consecutive winners, including all six races on the card at Chepstow on the first day of a two-day meeting. He was Champion Jockey on 26 occasions and had a record 4,870 winners in all, 14 of them in the Classics. In June 1953, however, that number was 13.

Richards had ridden the Derby 27 times, and had never won it. In 1942 he captured the 2,000 Guineas, the 1,000 Guineas, the St Ledger and the Oaks. Only the Derby had eluded him. In 1953, in what was to be his final full year of racing, and his last attempt at capturing the elusive prize, the recently knighted Richards' mount was the 5-1 joint favourite, Pinza.

Riding a smooth race all the way, he hit the front with two furlongs to go and stretched his lead comfortably to the line, accompanied by a thunder of applause and cheers, beating the Queen's horse, Aureole, into second. Having been crowned only four days earlier, it is unlikely she would have begrudged Richards his moment of glory. Interviewed afterwards, Sir Gordon Richards was asked how it felt finally to win the Derby, on this 28th attempt. 'Grand,' he replied. Pure class.

Of the 4,870 winners ridden by Sir Gordon Richards, whom many regard as the world's greatest ever jockey, his Derby victory in 1953 is surely his most famous.

Hogan's Command Performance

BEN HOGAN'S life story was so extraordinary that Hollywood made a film of it. His father, a blacksmith, committed suicide when Hogan was nine, perhaps even in front of the young boy, leaving the family in poverty. When Hogan took up golf he suffered from a hook and was never the greatest putter, but he created a swing and a focused persona that dominated the game.

By 1949, Hogan had won three Majors, but on a foggy night in February, his career and perhaps his life should have ended. Driving home, he was confronted head-on by a Greyhound bus and he threw himself across his wife to protect her. In so doing he avoided the steering column, which was driven back into his seat during the crash. Even so, his injuries were horrendous: walking seemed out of the question, never mind golf. Yet within a year he was playing again.

Then came the 1953 'Hogan Slam'. Masters won; US Open won; next the Open at Carnoustie. After two rounds he was two strokes off the lead, facing 36 holes in one day, a huge challenge given the pain he suffered in his legs. Undaunted, he produced near flawless golf, hitting 70 in the morning and a course record 68 in the afternoon to win by four shots. The first three Majors were his. Who knows what would have happened in the fourth if the USPGA had not clashed with the Open? The Scots dubbed him 'The Wee Ice Mon', but this iceman would not cometh again to the Open. One visit, one win.

Perfect preparation and four brilliant, ever-improving rounds of 73, 71, 70 and 68 made Ben Hogan's victory at Carnoustie in 1953 one of the most memorable Open Championships in golfing history.

Hungary Dismantle the Old Order

Ferenc Puskas (left) and Billy Wright lead the teams out for a match that would change the way football was played for ever.

WHETHER THIS was the 'Match of the Century' or the match that changed football, there is no doubting the lasting significance of Hungary's visit to Wembley on a drab November afternoon in 1953. England expected to win. Why wouldn't they? They had Matthews, Mortensen, and Billy Wright as captain and no team from outside the British Isles had ever beaten them at home.

But Hungary, the Olympic champions, pushed aside the predictable tactics and formations of the past. Wingers supported each other on the same wing; Hidegkuti, the centre forward, sat deep. The English players had no answer and often no one to mark, trudging off the pitch after 90 minutes on the wrong end of a 6-3 humiliation. The defining moment came in the 24th minute. Ferenc Puskas dragged the ball back with the studs of his boot, and left Wright sitting on the Wembley turf as the Hungarian fired home for 3-1.

Had England underestimated their opponents? Almost certainly. Had they underprepared? Perhaps. Was team selection, and Tom Finney's omission in particular, to blame?

Four months later in Budapest the world found out – Hungary 7 England 1. The consequences? Brazilian flair in the years to come, England's 'Wingless Wonders' (Alf Ramsey played that day at Wembley in 1953, scoring England's third from the penalty spot), Dutch 'Total Football', Gazza's tears (well, Bobby Robson was in the stands and the impression the gifted footballers made on him stuck with him throughout his career) and overall a new way of thinking about the game.

The Original Miracle Mile

THERE IS something essentially pure about the mile world record. It seems like Britain's distance; it's a race that's now only run on special occasions; and apart from anything else, it's one of the hardest world records to break. Hicham El Guerrouj's current landmark, of 3:43.13, was set back in 1999. In the nineteenth century, mile races were common and by the 1950s, crowds of up to 50,000 would turn up to watch at venues like White City. But it was on one magical spring day in leafy Oxford in 1954 that Roger Bannister became the name on every schoolchild's lips.

Time was a factor in more ways than one – John Landy was getting close to the four-minute landmark in Australia too – but plans were all in place on 6 May 1954, for an attempt by the Oxford University trio of Bannister, Chris Brasher and Chris Chataway, despite a strong side wind that almost caused Bannister to call it off. Brasher set the pace, with Bannister second and Chataway third: 57.5 seconds for the first lap, 1 minute 58 for the half-mile. Then it was Chataway's turn. Bannister had to run the last lap in 59 seconds, legs screaming, lungs bursting – his training was not as we know it. But with a supreme effort, kicking round the final bend, he reached the line. The time, 3:59.4 seconds (announced by Norris McWhirter, of all people), was drowned out by the cheers of the crowd. Not just sporting immortality, but for ever an inspiration: to Coe, Ovett and Cram, who would all hold the mile record, and to all runners everywhere.

Pacemaker Chris Chataway leads Roger Bannister around the third lap of the Iffley Road track on the way to the world's first sub-four-minute mile.

A Most Gallant Runner

ON A WINDLESS, sunny, 28°C afternoon, England's world record holder Jim Peters set off in the British Empire and Commonwealth Games marathon. His intention was to destroy the field and he did, as one after another of his fellow competitors, sometimes literally, fell by the wayside. Peters entered the Empire Stadium 17 minutes ahead of his nearest rival with 385 yards to go, but he was a spent force.

Severe dehydration and the effects of the heat had taken their toll. Minutes earlier, Roger Bannister had beaten John Landy in 'The Miracle Mile' (they were the only two men at that time to have broken four minutes) but Bannister could only look on in horror as Peters weaved across the track, stumbling, crawling, falling, clambering to his feet, falling again and again, in a gruesome parody of a drunk as he attempted to complete the race. In 11 minutes, he managed 200 yards. Eventually, with about 180 yards to go, one of the England team's medical staff, Mickey Mayes, stepped in, fearing for Peters' life. Delirious, Peters thought he had won.

Years later, in a demonstration of sportsmanship and dignity, Peters stated that his lasting grief was that his actions had robbed the eventual winner, Scotland's Jim McGhee (who himself had fallen a number of times), of the recognition he deserved. Peters never raced again. He received a medal from the Duke of Edinburgh inscribed with the words: 'J. Peters, a most gallant runner.' Richly deserved.

Jim Peters struggles to stay on his feet as he nears the finish line in the Empire Stadium in Vancouver. Moments later he collapsed.

GB Win First Rugby League World Cup

OVER THE YEARS the Rugby League World Cup has not had to look far to find trouble, with multiple format changes, intermittent public apathy and barren years when no tournament was staged at all. And as for unpredictability, the essence of sport, until 2008 only two teams, Great Britain and Australia, had ever won the trophy. Indeed only five teams have ever contested the final (and one of them was England in 1995, after the Great Britain team was split).

It was New Zealand who broke the GB/Australia duopoly in a controversial final against the Kangaroos in 2008, but back in the inaugural tournament (instigated by the French and itself suffering from a difficult conception) the Kiwis were no match for a makeshift Great Britain side who defeated them 26-6 in the group stage. Written off before the World Cup began, Great Britain went on to top the group on points difference above hosts France, with Australia third and New Zealand propping them all up.

The top two then met in the final in Paris, in a classic encounter that matched their earlier 13-13 tie in the group stage. Over 30,000 fans saw the French take a second half lead with a Cantoni try, but under the inspirational leadership of Dave Valentine, GB fought back to win 16-12 and lift the World Cup trophy. It's been a while since we last won it.

Great Britain's loose forward and skipper Dave Valentine bursts through a tackle during the first ever rugby league World Cup final against France.

Devon Loch – The Phantom Jumper

WHAT DID HAPPEN to Devon Loch and jockey Dick Francis with 50 yards to go in the 1956 Grand National? It certainly wasn't rider error; Francis was no slouch in the saddle, having been crowned Champion Jockey in 1954. So why did Devon Loch seemingly attempt a star jump and collapse on his stomach when clear of the field and within sight of the winning post, allowing ESB to charge past for the win? His owner, Her Majesty, Elizabeth the Queen Mother, who watched the race with her two daughters, had her own gracious explanation. 'That's racing,' she said afterwards. Other theories are rather more prosaic, including cramp, heart trouble and perhaps most likely, the shadow cast by the adjacent water jump spooking the horse into

Why it happened no one knows, but Devon Loch snatched defeat from the jaws of victory 50 yards short of the winning post at Aintree in 1956.

thinking there was a phantom fence to jump. Others still were more fanciful, such as a shock delivered from an underground electricity cable which came into contact with the horse's shoe, trapped wind as a result of a tight girdle or, best of all, a stun gun fired from the crowd. Francis himself put it down to one of two reasons. Either his mount just plain slipped or was distracted by the roar of the crowd as they prematurely celebrated the first royal victory since 1900, with hats and race cards flung into the air. Whatever the reason, there's a book in there somewhere ...

Trautmann – Breaks Neck, Wins Cup

HE HAD been a member of the Hitler Youth and a German paratrooper who saw action on the Soviet Front. He had been awarded the Iron Cross, had engineered escapes from the Allies, and been interned in a POW camp in Cheshire. He played for Manchester City and was the first goalkeeper to win the Football Writers' Player of the Year award ... Bert Trautmann did not have to do anything else to cement his place in football folklore.

But he did. Trautmann made 545 appearances for City and was a favourite with the fans, even though his signing (only three years after the war) was not initially universally popular. In the 1956 FA Cup final, City went 3-1 up in the 64th minute through a Jack Dyson goal made by Trautmann from his kick upfield after diving bravely to rob Birmingham attacker Eddy Brown of the ball.

A few minutes later, Trautmann was diving again, at the feet of Peter Murphy. Murphy's knee connected with Trautmann's neck. The big keeper lay still for a while before staggering to his feet, clearly in pain and badly concussed. With no substitutes allowed, Trautmann played on to huge cheers from the City supporters, and made important, match-winning saves. He was still rubbing his neck and holding it at an angle when he received his winners' medal from the Queen. A few days later he went for an X-ray, which revealed that the collision with Murphy had broken his neck.

Bert Trautmann saves bravely at the feet of Birmingham City's Peter Murphy – a save for which he was rewarded with a broken neck and a cup-winners' medal.

'A Very Great Piece of Bowling'

THE ASHES has produced some incredible stories over the years but one record that you can comfortably say will not be broken is the 19 wickets taken by Jim Laker at Old Trafford in 1956. It was the Fourth Test, but that hardly matters given the nature of the Surrey bowler's feat – does anyone remember the rest of that Ashes series?

For the record: the First and Fifth Tests were drawn, Australia won the Second at Lord's; in the Third Test a Peter May century, 11 Laker wickets and seven from fellow spinner Tony Lock had levelled the series at Headingley. Laker's performance at Old Trafford meant that England retained the urn they had captured for the first time in 19 years in 1953, winning the five-match series 2-1. Yet it was the metronomic nature of Laker's bowling that sticks in the memory.

England scored 459 in their first innings. Nine Australian wickets fell to Laker's off-breaks in their first innings as they slumped from 48 for 1 to 84 all out. Richie Benaud briefly offered some late-order resistance in the second innings but he was Laker's eighth of ten victims and when Len Maddocks was out lbw, Laker had match figures of 19 for 90. It was truly a different era – just look at the nonchalance with which England's Ashes hero walks off the pitch. Commentator John Arlott summed it up with admirable understatement when he said: '… and there are friends of mine who did not come today. They thought it would rain. Well it did look as if it was going to rain. They missed a very great piece of bowling.'

You wouldn't think it, judging from his expression, but Jim Laker (with jumper over his shoulder) leaves the Old Trafford pitch having taken all ten of Australia's second innings wickets.

Emerging from the Shadows

TO PLAY even a support role in one of the most enduring achievements in sport is an incredible feat; but to be always in that shadow, to never have your own recognition, could easily become a burden. Such was the potential fate of Chris Brasher, one of Roger Bannister's pacemakers for his historic four-minute mile (see page 31). But Brasher was made of sterner stuff. He set his sights on manufacturing his own moment in the sun and went about it with dedication, determination and attention to detail. His goal was the 1956 Olympics, and the less-than-fashionable 3,000 metres steeplechase, an event perhaps more suited to the bespectacled runner who bore only a passing resemblance to a traditional athlete. But what he might have lacked in natural talent he more than made up for in raw grit. He had a plan and he stuck to it, as he stuck to Hungarian Sandor Rozsnyoi as they approached the bell. Brasher hit the front at 300 metres as he had pre-appointed, cleared the last hurdle and crossed the line well ahead of the field only to discover, moments later, that his dream was being snatched away. A slight coming together with Norwegian Ernst Larsen, which had no detrimental impact, was deemed by the judges to warrant disqualification. With the full support of Rozsnyoi and Larsen (the athletes that had been moved up in the medals) Brasher appealed and won, carrying home Britain's first athletics gold for 20 years.

Chris Brasher takes the water jump at pace on his way to Olympic gold in the 1956 games in Melbourne.

TENNIS All England Lawn Tennis Championships
Ladies' Singles Final, Althea Gibson v. Darlene Hard, Wimbledon, London, 6 July 1957

1957

Althea Gibson: the Legacy Lives On

TO SAY Althea Gibson was a pioneer is like saying that Christopher Columbus enjoyed pottering around on the river. Columbus probably did, but he was much more than that. Equally, Gibson was a pioneer, but she also represented something far more important. She helped break down barriers that for far too long had seemed immovable.

On the evening of 7 July 1957, Gibson danced with Australian Lew Hoad at the Wimbledon champions' dinner, the first black player ever to step out on to that dance floor, having the day before defeated Californian Darlene Hard 6-3, 6-2 in the ladies' singles final. Gibson had not dropped a set in the entire tournament, only losing 30 games in total. Tall and athletic, she was favourite to win, having secured the French Open the previous year, along with the Wimbledon doubles title alongside Britain's Angela Buxton.

Gibson would go on to win the 1957 US Championship (as the US Open was known then), become World No. 1, and retain both titles the following year. Her achievements, remarkable in themselves, are all the more so because she was only able to pit herself against the best in her home country after she was permitted to enter the US Championship in 1950 – until then competitors could only qualify through points earned in all-white tournaments. Gibson's Grand Slam career may have ended in 1958, the year she turned professional in order to make a living, but her legacy lives on, not least in the brilliance of Venus and Serena Williams.

Althea Gibson, the first black tennis player to win Wimbledon, receives a congratulatory kiss from her vanquished opponent Darlene Hard.

Flight to Disaster

MANCHESTER UNITED were on their way home after a 3-3 draw with Red Star Belgrade had put them in the semi-final of the European Cup for the second successive year. Lying third in the league and in the fifth round of the FA Cup, the Busby Babes should have been about to come of age.

When United's chartered plane landed in Munich for refuelling, the snow was heavy and there was slush on the ground. On board, the mood was jovial, until after the second aborted take-off. By the time the party re-boarded following an engineering check, card games were put to one side and idle chatter was on hold. The plane never made it off the runway, ploughing through the airport perimeter fence, across a road and into a house. The tail and one wing were ripped off, the fuselage sliced in half.

Twenty-three of the 44 people on board died in the crash. Seven players died at the scene –

The BEA Elizabethan airliner, bringing the Manchester United players home from Yugoslavia, is a scene of devastation as it burns in a field near Munich airport after crashing and bursting into flames during an attempted take-off.

Geoff Bent, Roger Byrne, Eddie Colman, Mark Jones, David Pegg, Tommy Taylor and Billy Whelan. The magnificent Duncan Edwards died of his injuries 15 days later. Three members of the Manchester United staff also died, along with eight journalists, two crew members, a fan and a travel agent. Harry Gregg saved a pregnant woman and her baby. He and Bill Foulkes helped the injured. Jackie Blanchflower and Johnny Berry never played again. Matt Busby was kept alive in an oxygen tent and was twice given the last rites. He arrived back in Manchester 71 days later. The rebirth of the club seemed impossible. And yet it happened.

Part Three
1960 | 1969

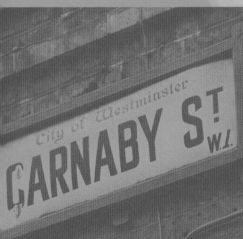

Football's 'Finest Hour'

Alfredo di Stefano (far left) and Ferenc Puskas (far right) lead the celebrations as Real Madrid win their fifth consecutive European Cup at Hampden Park.

IT WASN'T just Real Madrid's all-white strip that persuaded the Eintracht Frankfurt players that they were chasing ghosts on the evening of Wednesday 18 May 1960. Every one of the Madrid team, which included the glorious trio of Di Stefano, Puskas and Gento, glided, passed and anticipated moves as if they were other-worldly phantoms, untouchable and scary as hell, as they chased their fifth consecutive European Cup. And this was a Frankfurt side that had squeaked past a far-from-shabby Rangers side 12-4 on aggregate in the semi-final.

Incredibly, Di Stefano's hat-trick had to play second fiddle to a quadruple from Puskas: two left-footed bullets, a penalty and an agile header. The 127,621 fans crammed into Hampden Park witnessed one of the greatest football displays of all time, with the Spanish side recovering from 1-0

down to register a 7-3 victory. Among the throng were a number of young Scottish players and coaches, including a trainee striker from Queen's Park called Alex Ferguson, in attendance thanks to the allocation of tickets to their clubs.

Such was the impression made by this Real Madrid side that Scottish football was lifted to new heights for more than two decades, with Celtic, Rangers and Aberdeen lifting European trophies, and the national side regularly qualifying for the World Cup.

The Sledgehammer

IT'S NOT a bad thing to be remembered as the man who knocked Muhammad Ali to the floor. But that is the legacy of 'Our 'Enry', Henry Cooper, and ''Enry's 'Ammer', which put the legendary American down in the dying seconds of the fourth round of their non-title fight at Wembley in June 1963.

Controversy rages to this day over the fight, but what is certain is that Cooper was no 'bum', as the loudmouth American Cassius Clay called him in the run-up to the fight, and that he shocked Clay from the start of the bout. Sure, Cooper took the hits, and the cut above his left eye that was bad by the third round would eventually stop it in the fifth, just as Clay had (conveniently, for the conspiracy theorists) predicted. Clay was saved from hitting the canvas when his arm got caught in the ropes as he went down, and Angelo Dundee in Clay's corner allegedly used smelling salts after Cooper's left hook had hammered into his opponent's face. The subsequent delay in the fight is open to debate, a matter that became the subject of Henry's after-dinner speeches, to an extent. But the fire behind Clay's barrage of punches to win the contest was undeniable, and Cooper lost his golden chance at being the greatest.

He could not recreate it when the pair met again at Highbury in 1966, when Clay, by then Ali, was heavyweight champion of the world, and some world champion at that. But the original fight is now part of Wembley folklore. On the bout's 40th anniversary in 2003, Ali is alleged to have telephoned Cooper and said that he 'had hit [him] so hard that his ancestors in Africa felt it'.

He's there … bam … he's gone. Henry Cooper's sledgehammer punch is enough to put the mighty Cassius Clay on his backside.

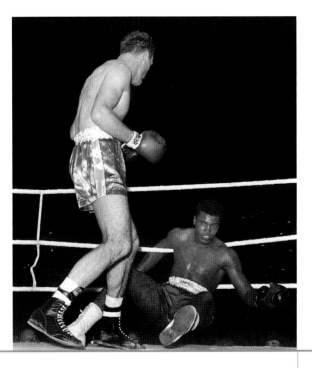

Arkle v. Mill House

ENGLAND V. IRELAND is always likely to stir sporting passion – never more so than at a race meeting, and with no greater intensity than at the Cheltenham Festival. In 1964, the thoroughbreds Mill House and Arkle represented the two nations. No one in England believed Mill House could be beaten. Winner of the Cheltenham Gold Cup in 1963 and conqueror of Arkle in the Hennessy Gold Cup that same season, surely it was a foregone conclusion. Sure, Arkle had shown some class in winning his debut chase at Cheltenham, but what did that matter? The big horse, Mill House, was unbeatable. Wasn't he?

Such was the hype and clear dominance of these two horses, that only two others entered the 1964 Cheltenham Gold Cup. They might as well have treated themselves to a lie-in. They had

no chance. With three fences to go, Pat Taaffe on Arkle was stalking Willie Robinson on Mill House. Over the third last and Mill House landed three lengths ahead. Over the second last, he landed just ahead. Over the last, Arkle landed a length in front. Mill House tried to respond, but Arkle was away, magnificent, the white star on his rival's forehead disappearing into the distance behind him as he glided over the turf to a five-length victory, breaking the track record by four seconds. The greatest steeplechase of all time had been run and the greatest steeplechaser of all time had arrived.

In a breathtaking race between the home nations' two finest thoroughbreds, Arkle took the lead going over the last fence to win the Gold Cup in a Cheltenham track record time.

Packer Upsets the Form Book

ANN PACKER very nearly didn't win Olympic gold. Not because she didn't have the sprint finish to reel in and then outpace the French runner Maryvonne Dupureur, but because she hadn't intended running in the 800 metres at all when she arrived in Tokyo for the 1964 Games.

Packer's preferred distance was the 400 metres, in which she had medal hopes. She eventually had to settle for silver in this event after perhaps giving too much in the qualifying rounds. She then watched her husband-to-be and GB team captain, Robbie Brightwell, finish fourth in the men's 400 metres final. His placing was perhaps partly due to the distraction of having to deal with a dispute between the team and the

British athletics authorities about the treatment of the athletes. Spurred on, Packer decided to give the 800 metres a go, despite only having run a few races at that distance.

She qualified as the slowest of the finalists, possibly learning from earlier mistakes. As a PE teacher and dedicated athlete, she was certainly fit enough to manage the three races required for each event and, as she crossed the finishing line of the 800 metres in a world record time of 2:01.1, to the cheers of her teammates and fiancé, she barely looked out of breath. And that was it, her last race. She retired aged 22, married Brightwell (who won silver in the 4 x 400 metres relay) and raised a family of three sons, two of whom went on to become professional footballers with Manchester City.

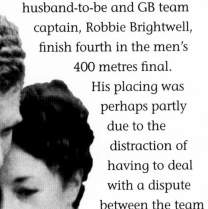

(Left) The Posh and Becks of their day? Robbie Brightwell congratulates his girlfriend Ann Packer on her Olympic 800 metres gold, a race she won in a world record time (above).

England – Champions of the World

BY THE day of the final, most of the questions posed by the World Cup tournament had been answered. Would the trophy be found? Yes, thanks to Pickles. Were the hosts genuine contenders after the dour 0-0 against Uruguay in which England failed to score at Wembley for the first time in 28 years? Yes, as the tournament progressed so did the quality of their performances. Would Alf Ramsey stick with genuine wingers? No. Would Nobby Stiles play any further part following his rash challenge on Jacques Simon? Yes, but only after Ramsey threatened to resign if he was instructed not to pick him. Would Jimmy Greaves play again after he recovered from a gashed shin sustained in the French game? No.

Could North Korea, the unlikely conquerors of Italy, overcome the brilliance of Eusebio and the Portuguese to reach the semi-finals? No, but only

England's World Cup final triumph was fashioned by the West Ham trio of Peters (above) and Hurst (below right), who supplied the goals, and skipper Bobby Moore (top right), who supplied calm assurance and leadership at the back to lift the famous trophy for the only time in the nation's history.

after Portugal clawed themselves back from 3-0 down. Would the English players survive their quarter-final battle with the fiery Argentinians? Yes, with a Geoff Hurst header. Were Eusebio and his teammates a bridge too far for the wingless wonders? No, Bobby Charlton saw to that with his greatest game ever in an England shirt.

Only a few questions remained. Such as: how to prepare for the biggest football game in the nation's history? With a trip to the local cinema to watch *The Blue Max*, featuring a First World War German pilot hell-bent on shooting down Allied aircraft. According to Alf Ramsey, anyway.

'You have won it once. Now go and win it again.'

Tactics were going to be critical. Franz Beckenbauer was the danger man and Ramsey sacrificed his most lethal attacking force, Bobby Charlton, with the instruction to shadow and neutralise the young German. Hurst was preferred to Greaves and wingers were cast aside in favour of an Alan Ball–Martin Peters combination.

A rare error by Ray Wilson led to the German opening goal, which was quickly nullified by a West Ham special, delivered by Bobby Moore and finished by Hurst. Fortunately, Peters then beat Jack Charlton to a loose ball to put England ahead,

until the 90th minute when a still-disputed free kick was driven towards the English goal, ricocheted in the box and Wolfgang Weber squeezed it home.

Then came extra time and Ramsey's genius. He urged his players to remain on their feet, to give no sense they were flagging, and delivered his classic line. 'You have won it once. Now go and win it again.' They did. Who knows whether Hurst's strike bounced on or over the line? It didn't matter as he went on to ensure victory with an apparent attempt to boot the ball as far into the crowd as possible. It was all over then.

Jock the Giant-Killer

Berwick goalkeeper-manager Jock Wallace snatches the ball off the heads of the Rangers forwards as the Second Division side pulled off a sensational victory in the first round of the Scottish Cup.

IT WAS not a good year for Rangers FC. In 1967 their great rivals, Celtic, became the first British club to win the European Cup six days before Rangers themselves could have tasted European victory had they not failed to produce what they were capable of against a lesser Bayern Munich side in the European Cup-Winners' Cup final. On the domestic front, Celtic also won the Treble.

For the 'Gers, the most notable event of the season was the worst defeat in the club's history when they were knocked out of the Scottish Cup in the first round by Second Division Berwick Rangers. A record crowd of 13,365 turned up at the only Scottish League ground in England to witness the Glasgow side batter the Berwick goal to no avail. Berwick had taken the lead through Sammy Reid and thereafter gave all they had in defence to keep the visitors at bay. Incredibly, they managed it, in a game the legendary John Greig described as the greatest embarrassment of his career.

Unknown at the time, however, there were two small consolations for Rangers that day. The first is that they were introduced to the manager who would win them two domestic Trebles – the Berwick goalie Jock Wallace, who kept the marauding Rangers forwards at bay with a string of spectacular saves. The second? This result is no longer the most shocking upset in Scottish football. That is one title Rangers have been more than glad to pass on to Celtic FC (see page 66).

The Lisbon Lions Are Kings of Europe

IF IT hadn't been for Tommy Gemmell, the first British side to win the European Cup might have all come from within 12 miles of Celtic Park. Ten of them did, but Gemmell was from Saltcoats, 30 miles away. It is an astonishing fact, never to be repeated. On a summer's evening, in a stadium near Lisbon, the local boys made good. The Lisbon Lions defeated the might of Internazionale of Milan. In the run-up, the Italians may have thought it was men versus boys. Manager Jock Stein, the Celtic players and the 12,000 fans who travelled to Portugal by plane, train and automobile certainly didn't. This was creativity versus negativity. The Italians scored a penalty after seven minutes and attempted to shut up shop. The Celts poured forward, overlapping full backs Gemmell

and Craig tantalising alongside the brilliance of wingers Lennox and the wonder that was Jimmy Johnstone. On 63 minutes the Celtic full backs combined and Gemmell blasted home. Five minutes from full time, Scottish ambition broke Italian resistance as Murdoch's shot was steered home by Chalmers. At the final whistle, the pitch became a sea of green and white as fans swept on in good-natured celebration to watch captain Billy McNeill lift the trophy. Alone. His teammates had been unnecessarily held in the dressing room for their safety. It didn't matter. Jock Stein and Celtic were champions. The party lasted a long time.

Arms are raised all round as Celtic become the first British club to win the European Cup.

Tommy Simpson Dies on Mont Ventoux

BRITISH CYCLING has had many heroes down the years, and despite his controversial approach to the sport, you won't hear many bad words about Tommy Simpson. The first Briton to wear the yellow jersey in the Tour de France, Simpson then became Britain's first world road racing champion, as well as winning the Milan–San Remo and the Paris–Nice races. His achievements made him British cycling's first celebrity.

Simpson was renowned for pushing himself to the absolute limit, beyond the pain barrier, and that intensity of effort would often involve the use of amphetamines, not to mention fairly frequent slugs of brandy – water was, unbelievably, rationed for racers in those days. It was a combination of the drugs and the unrelenting sun on the punishing slopes of the 6,000-foot high Mont Ventoux that did for Simpson in 1967. It was the 13th stage of the Tour, it was Friday the 13th, and after falling off his bike, he managed to continue for another 300 metres before collapsing once more.

Simpson died in Avignon hospital. He died young, but he lived fast enough to become an enduring legend. A memorial stands at the foot of the mountain that killed him. It is a place at which all passing cyclists pay homage.

Lived fast, died young – Tommy Simpson was Britain's first cycling celebrity.

Heaven and Hell

IT IS reasonable to assume that Jim Clark had strong views about Monza. In 1961, Clark was involved in a collision with Count Wolfgang von Trips during the first lap. The German driver's Ferrari mounted a small bank lined with onlookers, and spun into the air. Von Trips and 14 spectators lost their lives in one of the most terrible accidents in Formula One history.

Six years later, at a modified track, Clark was in pole position and led until suffering a puncture at the halfway stage. By the time he replaced the tyre, he was a lap down. Giving his Lotus 49 everything he had, Clark weaved his way through the pack and, incredibly, retook the lead. On the final lap Clark was on the brink of a monumental win when he ran out of petrol. Surtees and Brabham surged on and Clark spluttered home in third place. Clark may not

Jim Clark gives the thumbs up to yet another chequered flag, this time for winning the Grand Prix at Watkins Glen, New York, in 1967.

have worn the winning laurel wreath on the podium that day, but it was a heavenly drive which he followed up with wins in the US and the Mexico Grands Prix to record third place in the Championship.

It was his last ever full season in motor racing as he was killed in a Formula Two accident in Hockenheim, Germany, in April 1968. In tribute, his great friend and mentor Colin Chapman said of him, 'His most profound influence was not as a racing driver, but his success as a man.' Given that Jim Clark, twice world champion in 1963 and 1965 and winner of 25 Grands Prix, was perhaps the greatest driver of all time, this is perhaps the greatest compliment of all.

1968

The 'Poor Lad'

HALF AN hour before the start of the 1968 Challenge Cup final, the Wembley turf was still 'hallowed'. By the time Leeds and Wakefield Trinity kicked off, it had become marshland following a torrential downpour. The resulting conditions for the 'Watersplash Final' may not have been conducive to free-flowing play, but they contributed to one of the most exciting and dramatic finals ever.

With the score 11-7 and barely a minute to go, Leeds looked to have the trophy firmly in their wet hands, until Wakefield's Ken Hirst outpaced the opposition defence to touch down between the posts to make it 11-10. A simple conversion to win it. Fifteen yards out, the highly talented and prolific goal-kicker Don Fox placed

Don Fox is consoled by his teammates after missing the simplest of kicks and condemning Wakefield to the dreaded runners-up spot.

his ball in the mud, took a few steps back, paused, then took his run-up. The Leeds players behind the posts either hung their heads in defeat or couldn't bear to watch.

As Fox swung his right boot, his standing foot slipped, he sliced the kick and the ball looped lamely past the right-hand post. The Leeds players leapt in startled joy, Fox collapsed to his knees, and the referee blew the final whistle. Five minutes before, Fox had been named man of the match. The irony was lost on no one. As ever, commentator Eddie Waring summed it up best: 'He's a poor lad.'

The 'Holy Grail' Secured

TEN YEARS after the horrors of Munich, two survivors of the crash, Bill Foulkes and Bobby Charlton, took to the Wembley field in the final of the European Cup. A third survivor, Matt Busby, masterminded his beloved United's endeavours from the dugout.

Standing in their way was Eusebio's Benfica: skilful, hard opponents. An early strike by the Portuguese talisman beat Alex Stepney, but not the bar, and gave ample warning that sentimentality had no role in the proceedings. In the era before substitutes, an injury to the Benfica right-back Adolfo gave United an advantage down that flank, and in the 53rd minute they exploited it when Charlton headed home a David Sadler cross. A well-worked equaliser from Graça brought Benfica level and with ten minutes to go, Eusebio broke through on goal. Stepney stood firm and was rewarded with genuine appreciative applause from the striker.

Extra time saw the Portuguese flag as United took control. After three minutes, George Best stole the ball from a hesitant defender to walk it round the goalkeeper and in. Best at his best. A minute later birthday-boy Brian Kidd headed in the killer blow, with Charlton sweeping home his second in the 99th minute to complete Matt Busby's version of the holy grail. At the final whistle, the emotion poured out of them all, especially Charlton, Foulkes and Busby. They had been on a long road that stretched back to a snowy German runway.

United's David Sadler models the new European Cup hat amidst euphoric scenes following their Wembley triumph against Benfica.

Gary Sobers Hits Sporting Perfection

IF YOU had been at Glamorgan's St Helen's ground on Saturday 31 August 1968, you would have witnessed sporting perfection. Playing for Nottinghamshire in a county game and facing Malcolm Nash, Gary Sobers hit every ball of an over for six, a unique achievement at the time. You can't beat 36 off an over. Overthrows and no-balls don't count. It is perfection.

Sobers came in to bat with Nottinghamshire on 308 for 5. He was looking for quick runs and a declaration. The historic moment came when the West Indian was 40 not out. Nash, normally a seamer, decided to go for left-arm spin. Not a good decision. The first two deliveries were thumped out of the ground. The third went over mid-off and the fourth over backward square leg.

Sobers was the first batsman ever to hit six sixes in an over in first-class cricket. It was 16 years before anyone was able to match him, when Ravi Shastri repeated the trick for Bombay against Baroda.

There was drama with the fifth ball. Sobers didn't hit it cleanly and it flew towards Roger Davis on the boundary. He caught it but stumbled over the rope. The previous season, Sobers would have been out. He began to walk, only stopping when no finger was raised. A new rule had been introduced. If the ball was caught but the fielder then went outside the boundary, not out. Nash tried seam for number six but that too soared out of the ground, and with a raise of his bat to acknowledge the cheers of the crowd, Sobers made his declaration on 394 for 5, of which Sobers had made 76 not out.

Beamon's Leap of the Century

SPECTATORS IN the Olympic Stadium, Mexico City, on 18 October 1968, really did believe that man could fly. In a period of six seconds, in his first attempt in the long jump final, the American athlete Bob Beamon soared into history, destroying not only the previous long jump world record by an astonishing 21¾ inches (55cm) but also the official measuring equipment which was not designed for this length of jump.

The officials took 20 minutes to announce the distance, eventually having to measure it manually. Unfamiliar with metric conversion, when Beamon saw 8.90 metres flash up on the scoreboard he wasn't sure what it meant. When his teammate (and then world record holder) Ralph Boston, explained that this was 29 feet, 2½ inches, the emotion consumed Beamon, his legs gave way and he collapsed. None of the other athletes came anywhere near the mark and so it remained until the record was broken in 1991 by fellow American Mike Powell.

The impact of the Leap of the Century was widespread. The defining image of the jump was taken by a British accountant called Tony Duffy, who had aspirations to become a professional photographer. Having captured Beamon in mid-flight, he was so inspired he quit his day job and decided to give it a go. He went on to establish Allsport, one of the most highly regarded sports photo agencies in the world.

Bob Beamon's 8.90-metre jump at the 1968 Mexico City Games shocked everyone, Beamon included. It was a world record that stood for 23 years.

The Closest Race in History

IN 1968 Jackie Stewart turned down the chance to drive for Ferrari, opting instead to race for a new, private entrant on the Formula One circuit – Ken Tyrrell. In a team led by Tyrrell out of a wood yard in Ockham, Surrey, and with the backing of the French companies Matra and Elf, Stewart won three Grands Prix but narrowly missed out on the World Championship to Graham Hill.

In 1969 he went one better in a season of brilliant driving in a Matra MS80. After five wins in the first seven races (including the French Grand Prix, at which he was the first driver to celebrate a Formula One victory by spraying champagne), Stewart knew that a win in Monza would secure the title. Despite Ferrari's poor season the Italian circuit was packed to the rafters to witness one of the most exhilarating Grand Prix races of all time, one that saw four

In 1969 Jackie Stewart – the 'Flying Scotsman'– really hit his stride, winning six of the 11 Grands Prix to win his first world championship.

cars come out of the last bend in contention, speeding flat out towards the chequered flag. As Jochen Rindt, Jean-Pierre Beltoise and Bruce McLaren changed up the gears from third to fifth, Stewart was able to hold his car in fourth, critically giving him less than a fraction of a second, literally inches, of advantage and his first world title. The result – still regarded as the closest 1, 2, 3, 4 in the history of Formula One with only 0.19 of a second between first and fourth – was only decided via a photo finish.

For Stewart, the champagne was already becoming a bit of a habit.

Jack Nicklaus – Supreme Sportsman

BY 1969 the US dominance of the Ryder Cup had transformed the contest into something of an irrelevance to the Americans, or at best a goodwill event. Royal Birkdale in September changed all that, reigniting the Cup as a sporting challenge and a competition of sportsmanship.

By the last afternoon, with eight singles left to play, Britain were 13-11 ahead. The recent Open champion, Tony Jacklin, was paired with Jack Nicklaus in the final match, having already beaten him 4 & 3 that morning. As they stood on the 18th green, after Jacklin had sunk a 50-foot eagle putt on the 17th to go all square, the overall match score read 15½ each. Both on the green in two, Jacklin's ball was 30 feet from the pin, with Nicklaus well inside. If Jacklin could hole another monster, the pressure would be on the American,

but his effort was 2 feet short. The Golden Bear pushed his putt almost 5 feet past but kept his nerve on the return to sink the putt.

As he stooped for his ball, he picked up Jacklin's marker, conceding the putt, and halving both the match and, for the first time in history, the Ryder Cup (which the American team therefore retained). As they shook hands, the American explained, 'I didn't think you would miss it, but I didn't want to give you the opportunity.'

Supreme skill, drama, tension and sportsmanship at a stroke – players today would do well to remember this glorious moment.

Jack Nicklaus shakes hands with Tony Jacklin – a moment to restore even the most hardened cynic's faith in the beauty of sporting competition.

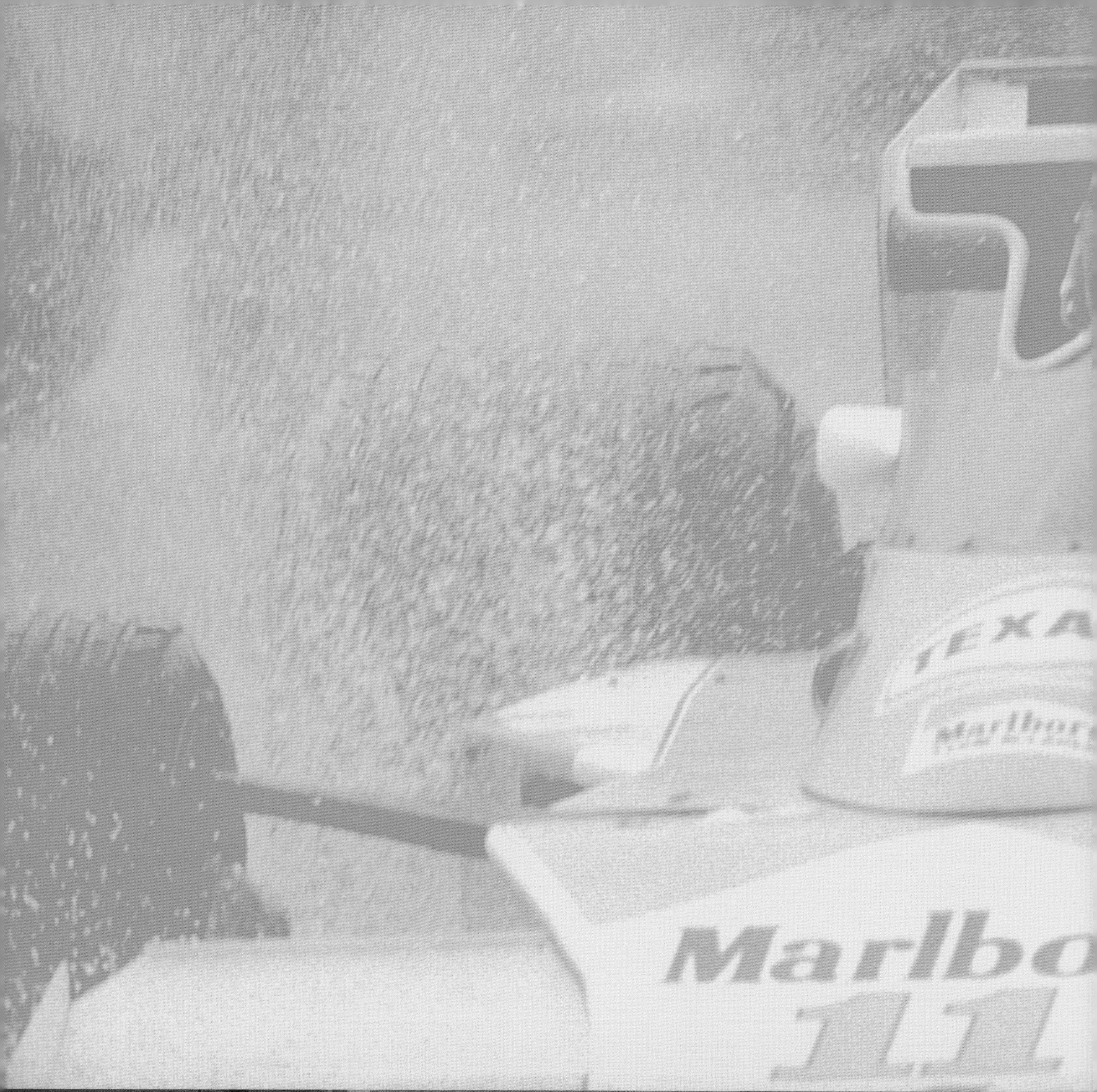
TEXA
Marlbo
11

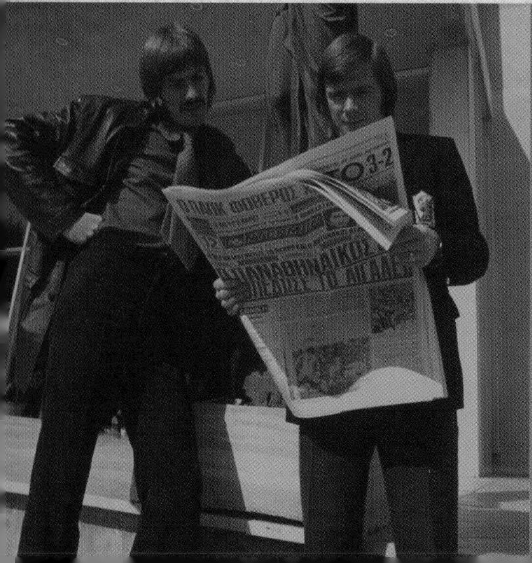

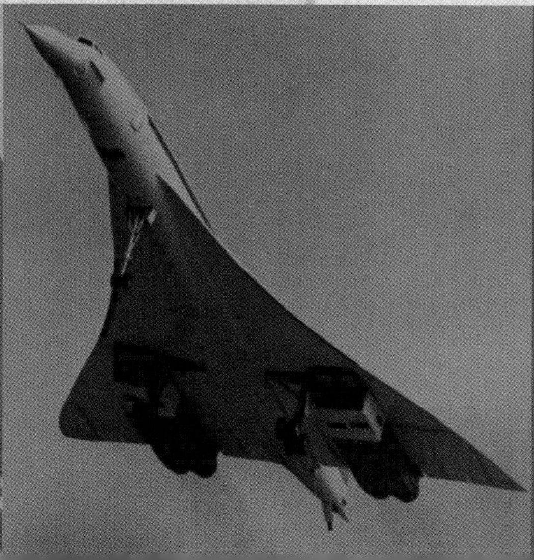

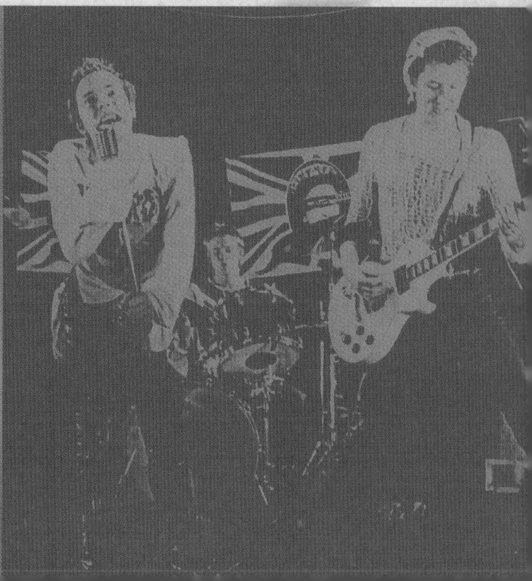

Part Four
1970 | 1979

A Very English Result

IS IT strange that we should remember a defeat as one of England's greatest ever games? Was it just the advent of colour TV, a sense of hedonism and the exoticism of Mexico that made the 1970 World Cup extra special? Or was it the fact that when England played Brazil in the searing heat and energy-sapping altitude of Guadalajara, it was a meeting between the world's best two teams, and a match played in the very best spirit of sportsmanship (easier in the group stages, of course). And, again oddly, the game will for ever live on for two brilliant pieces of defence.

After England had looked the better team in the first half, passing beautifully, arguably better than in 1966, Jairzinho's cross to Pele was inch-perfect. Pele's leap stupendous. Gordon

Skippers Carlos Alberto (left) and Bobby Moore pose together before one of the finest matches of England's footballing history.

Banks's save just out of this world. Then after Jairzinho had scored with a thumping drive from Pele's neat set-up, Brazil were on the break once again. Carlos Alberto's long ball, Jairzinho streaking forward, only Bobby Moore and Brian Labone back. And there was Moore's exquisitely timed tackle, a model for all defenders down the generations. At the other end, Jeff Astle with a golden chance, blazed wide. It was a very English result – glory extracted from defeat – and it didn't get any better. West Germany in the quarter-final. Peter Bonetti in goal. We don't need to go there. But we do remember Brazil.

The 'Best Week' of Tony Jacklin's Life

IT WAS a good day for compelling, convincing and historic sporting wins. In Mexico City, Brazil produced perhaps the best football ever seen to demolish Italy 4-1 in the World Cup final. Almost 2,000 miles north, in Chaska, Minnesota, Tony Jacklin became the first British winner of the US Open since Willie Macfarlane in 1925, leading from day one and winning by a comprehensive seven strokes over American Dave Hill. Not that it was all plain sailing during the final round.

Bogies on the seventh and eighth put a dent in Jacklin's seemingly impregnable armour and gave Hill, now only three behind, something to aim at. Was Jacklin crumbling under the pressure? The ninth and tenth gave the answer. The Scunthorpe lad produced consecutive birdies, including a monster putt on the ninth, effectively ending any possible challenge. Armour fully repaired, Jacklin completed his round with a swashbuckling 25-foot putt for a birdie. He later called the whole experience, 'The best week of golf I have ever had in my life.'

The significance of both events that June day was not lost on those back home. Pele and his teammates were hailed in Brazil as all-conquering heroes, displaying the Jules Rimet trophy, which was theirs for ever. Back in Jacklin's hometown, in recognition of his achievement, well-wishers lined the streets to cheer a victory cavalcade, headed by the man himself in a vintage Cadillac. Beats an open-topped bus tour any day.

Jacklin celebrates in style, driving through the streets of his hometown, Scunthorpe, in a pink Cadillac after winning the US Open.

The Brilliant Brazilians

FOR DRAMA, and other rather obvious reasons, the 1966 World Cup final is hard to beat. But for the football purists, you can hardly look further than 1970 in Mexico when the brilliant Brazilians capped a wonderful tournament by blitzing four goals past Italy. In so doing, and becoming three-time winners, the Jules Rimet trophy was theirs to keep. Latin American pride was at its most exuberant: 'The country laughed and the people danced,' as the unlikely figure of Franz Beckenbauer admitted.

Everything about Brazil's victory in the final seemed so fitting, from Pele scoring the opening goal to Carlos Alberto the captain netting the last, the most often replayed, from the No. 10's perfectly weighted pass. And yet Pele had almost been dropped before the tournament, with the manager Joao Saldanha wary of the physical threat posed by European sides. But Saldanha was sacked, and his replacement, Mario Zagallo, instead let the football breathe with an exhilarating counter-attacking style: Tostao up front, Rivelino on the left, Jairzinho on the right. They had guile, skill and speed all in abundance. Brazil scored 19 goals in their six games during the tournament, and all seven of their scorers were involved in the last one. It was football at its life-affirming best.

Captain Fantastic: Carlos Alberto, captain of the finest team ever, scorer of the winning goal in the finest ever World Cup final – it doesn't get much better than that – even Pele (left) enjoyed it..

A Tragedy Waiting to Happen

IN 1971, the traditional Old Firm New Year fixture was played on a cold, dreich Saturday afternoon. For 89 minutes, the 80,000 spectators witnessed a game to match the conditions, until Jimmy Johnstone put Celtic 1-0 up. Many Rangers fans began to head home to warmth and the last remains of festive cheer. Less than a minute later, and with almost the last kick of the match, Colin Stein dramatically equalised.

Initially this late flurry of action was 'blamed' for the tragedy that followed, rumours circulating that departing fans had turned back to celebrate, resulting in the fatal crush. The subsequent inquiry put this falsehood to bed. When the steel barriers on Stairway 13 collapsed, the spectators were all heading out of the stadium. In the melee of bodies caused by the incident, 66 people lost their lives. Many more were injured. The players knew nothing of the dreadful events unfolding as they left the pitch and made their way up the tunnel to change. Both areas would soon be strewn with stretchers bearing bodies covered with sheets. Ambulance crews and nurses tried desperately to save as many people as they could.

Nothing can take away from the grief of the families who lost loved ones, but one small piece of solace may be found in the fact that the subsequent redevelopment of Ibrox proved to be the template for safety standards in football stadiums following the horrors of Hillsborough many years later.

Stairway 13 reveals its ugly truth the day after the tragic events of 2 January 1971 when 66 fans lost their lives here.

Double Joy for Arsenal

CHARLIE GEORGE. The name evokes an era. The 1970s. Long hair, flares and sideburns. Booze, birds and bookies. The footballers of the time, the likes of Frank Worthington, Peter Osgood and Stan Bowles, were badly behaved but brilliant on the field, and looked as if they didn't care much about anything. But they wanted to win and Charlie George, a local boy and Arsenal fan, had his day in the sun in 1971, stretched out on the Wembley turf after scoring the winner against Liverpool deep into extra time in the FA Cup final.

The shot itself, arrowed past Ray Clemence from the edge of the area, is remembered less than George's iconic celebration, which in turn can obscure the significance of the goal. It sealed the Double – a huge deal for the north London club. It was not just Arsenal's first Double, more importantly it got them level with Spurs, who had secured the first League and Cup combination of the century ten years earlier. Frank McLintock, the inspirational captain of Bertie Mee's team, held aloft his second trophy in a week. George, just 20 at the time, would never hit such heights again, but he had the ultimate experience for the fan turned player and made himself a genuine Arsenal legend.

Local boy makes good: Charlie George scores the unforgettable second goal to seal the Double for Arsenal.

A Break in the Clouds

THE NAMES are legendary: JPR Williams, David Duckham, Barry John, Gareth Edwards, Ian McLauchlan, Willie John McBride, Fergus Slattery. With players like these in a squad with a backbone of the Grand Slam-winning Welsh side, the 1971 Lions had a great chance to break their New Zealand duck. Orchestrated in a near-professional manner by manager Dr Doug Smith, coached by the visionary Carwyn James and led by Welsh skipper John Dawes, the tourists were determined to exorcise the demons of the 4-0 whitewash in 1966.

The Lions' brutal encounter with Canterbury demonstrated their intent. Prop Sandy Carmichael had his cheekbone broken by a punch but they stood firm to win. Playing throughout the tour as a tight unit, individuals stepped up when it mattered. In the First Test,

The 1971 Lions team became the first to win a series in New Zealand in almost three-quarters of a century of trying.

it was 'Mighty Mouse' McLauchlan with a charge-down try; Gerald Davies' two late tries after the Second Test was clearly lost gave the Lions faith; the Third Test was all about Barry John, with two converted tries and a drop goal sealing a 13-3 victory.

So to the Fourth and final Test, a nervous encounter that saw New Zealand pegged back from 8-0 up to 11-11. Step forward JPR. From 45 metres, he landed his one and only drop goal. The All Blacks fought back to square the match, but not the series.

A shift in hemispheric power? No, just a break in the clouds as the Kiwis haven't lost a series since.

Celtic Stung by Unpredictable Thistle

Too little too late, as Kenny Dalglish scrambles in the Hoops' only goal during an afternoon where there were plenty of red Celtic faces.

FRANK BOUGH was flustered. Surely that cutting edge of technology, the teleprinter, ticking out the half-time score from Hampden was for once producing inaccurate information? Partick Thistle 4 Celtic 0. 'We'll check that for you,' he said. 'That might be wrong.'

Earlier, on *Football Focus*, the preview of the match had stated, 'It's League Cup final day at Hampden Park, where Celtic meet Partick Thistle, who have no chance.' Celtic, after all, had been in the European Cup final the previous year. For their part, Thistle had just been promoted to the First Division and included a teacher, a student and an electrician in their line-up.

Yet, after 37 minutes, an Alex Rae volley, a Bobby Lawrie curler, a Denis McQuade scrambled effort and a Jimmy Bone tap-in

meant the game was over. Well, not quite. This was Thistle after all. No one was ruling out a 6-4 Celtic victory, apart perhaps from thousands of Rangers fans pouring into Hampden at half-time to enjoy their arch-rival's misery.

But the Jags held on, a Kenny Dalglish effort their only blemish, to achieve one of the greatest upsets in Scottish, British, even world, football. On the final whistle, the commentator, Arthur Montford, announced with confidence, 'A magnificent performance by Thistle, who have finally, once and for all, and emphatically, put paid to the unpredictable tag.' A week later they lost 7-2 to Aberdeen.

That Radford Moment

AH, THE magic of the FA Cup! It's something that can be difficult to conjure up these days, but back in the era of muddy pitches and genuine giant killers, it really was there in abundance. For most people, Ronnie Radford's long-range screamer past Willie McFaul for Hereford against Newcastle is not just one of those special *Match of the Day* moments, but the definitive FA Cup goal – just what the competition is all about.

Southern League Hereford had held Newcastle to a 2-2 draw at St James' Park after the third round tie had twice been postponed, and more

rain led to the replay being called off three more times. It finally went ahead on a cold, windy, foggy day, on a suitably terrible pitch. The Hereford dream seemed over when 'Supermac' Malcolm Macdonald headed the First Division visitors into the lead. Then came Radford's moment, immortalised in the new young BBC commentator John Motson's words – 'Radford again … oh what a goal, what a goal, Radford the scorer …' – as the Parka-wearing fans invaded the pitch in celebration. It is often forgotten that Radford's goal was not the winner – substitute Ricky George sealed the match in extra time – but this is one FA Cup goal that will simply never be forgotten. Of course, Hereford lost to West Ham in the next round, but no one can take away from the glory of that 40-yard screamer!

(Above left) Hereford scorers Ronnie Radford (top left) and Ricky George (middle left) celebrate the non-leaguers historic FA Cup win over Newcastle. Radford's equaliser and his subsequent celebration (above) have become part of *Match of the Day* history.

Sport v. Politics

(Above) Mary Peters (centre), a 33-year-old secretary from Belfast, won Britain's only athletics gold at the Munich Games. (Below) The defining image of an event that realised the International Olympic Committee's worst fears.

ALTHOUGH CHIEFLY REMEMBERED for the horror of what has since become known as the Munich massacre, in which 11 Israeli athletes were killed by members of the Palestinian terrorist group Black September, the XXth Olympiad was also memorable for a number of incredible sporting achievements. Who can forget the charm of Olga Korbut in the gymnastics, the grit of Lasse Viren of Finland in the 5,000 and 10,000 metres and the extraordinary basketball final in which the Soviet Union beat the USA in overtime, a result the USA refused to accept? But two other stars also stood out.

American swimmer Mark Spitz contested seven events over eight days: 100 metres freestyle, 200 metres freestyle, 100 metres butterfly, 200 metres butterfly, 4 x 100 metres freestyle relay, 4 x 200 metres freestyle relay, 4 x 100 metres medley relay. He won seven golds with seven world records. And all done with a 'tache that surely wasn't aquadynamic. It was an incredible

performance, only bettered by Michael Phelps in the 2008 Beijing Games. Spitz was required to leave the Games for security reasons before the closing ceremony, as it was thought that he might be an additional target for the terrorists because of his Jewish heritage. He would surely have been greeted by the crowd as one of the greatest Olympians of all time.

Belfast was in need of some good news in the summer of 1972 and its adopted daughter, Mary Peters, provided it. Born on Merseyside, Peters moved to Northern Ireland as a young girl and in Munich she was competing in her third Olympics. At 33 years old, this was surely her last chance at pentathlon gold, having been placed fourth in the event in 1964 and ninth in 1968.

Up against local heroine, Heide Rosendahl, who had already won long jump gold, Peters knew she would have to be on top form. On day one she was, with three personal bests: 100 metres hurdles, shot putt and high jump. In the lead going into day two, Peters then disappointed in the long jump. Everything hinged on the 200 metres, one of Rosendahl's best events, which she duly won, giving the German 4,791 points and a new world record.

Peters had come fourth in the race with yet another PB. The position didn't matter though; it was all about the time. Was 24.08 sufficient? Minutes ticked by as the scores were calculated. The BBC thought she had it, but no one was sure. Then came the announcement. 'Mary Peters of Great Britain, 4,801.' Another new world record, and one that still stands.

Sport or politics? It's not that hard a choice.

Sustem Reuther

Despite the horrific massacre of the Israeli hostages and their captors, the Munich Games are also remembered for incredible sporting performances from athletes such as Olga Korbut (above), who won three gymnastic golds, and Mark Spitz (left), who won seven golds and broke seven world records in the swimming events.

Rugby's Greatest Try ... Really!

Tom David (left) passes the ball to Derek Quinnell despite being well collared by New Zealand's JF Karam in the run-up to rugby's finest try, scored by Gareth Edwards.

IT HAS been described as the greatest try ever scored, and for once that seems no exaggeration. When the All Blacks took to the Cardiff Arms Park field in January 1973 to take on the Barbarians, there was a massive sense of expectation. International matches were far more scarce back then, but as remains the case now, the Baa-Baas were renowned for their carefree, attacking play. Even better, many of them were Welsh – the stars of that decade of British rugby – and playing in front of home fans who were as always in good voice.

The game got underway with a flurry of exchanges at breakneck speed, and then the ball was retrieved by fly-half Phil Bennett close to his own line. The rest of the move has become engraved on rugby consciousness. Three superb, swerving sidesteps by Bennett. They could have been greeted with olés! To Williams, Pullin, John Dawes, then the dummy. Arguably the best move of all, by Tom David, offloading the ball to Derek Quinnell for a fantastic take. And then Gareth Edwards, bursting from deep, up the left touchline, to dive headlong and score in the corner. Brilliant, just brilliant.

Oh, and the final score ... the Barbarians won 23-11.

'We May Not be Much Good, but at Least We Turn Up'

AS JOHN PULLIN led England out at Lansdowne Road in February 1973 his side were on a losing streak of seven matches in the Championship. At the end of the 80 minutes, that run had been extended to eight after they lost 18-9. Not that it really mattered. This match represented more than the accumulation of points from tries, conversions and penalties. What counted, as Pullin said in his speech at the after-match party, was that England turned up.

The early 1970s marked the height of the Troubles in Northern Ireland, and the previous season's tournament had to be abandoned when Scotland and Wales refused to travel to Dublin for fear of terrorist attack. The fact that England, of all countries, chose to defy the potential threat and play meant a lot to the Irish, and they displayed their sentiments in the most glorious fashion.

As England emerged on to the pitch, the 50,000 supporters in the stadium rose as one to their feet to welcome them with a thunderous five-minute ovation. It is often said that sport and politics should never mix, but sometimes it is inevitable and sometimes it is for the best.

John Pullin, a teak-tough farmer from Bristol, led England with distinction through an admittedly bleak period for English rugby.

Stokoe's Gallop for Glory

Sunderland's Ian Porterfield (in stripes, second from right) smacks home one of the most popular ever FA Cup final goals against Don Revie's mighty Leeds United.

BY 1973, Don Revie's Leeds United had won just about everything there was to win in football: League champions, FA Cup holders, League Cup winners, two European trophies in the cabinet. They had a line-up that struck fear into the hearts of opponents: Lorimer, Bremner, Giles, Madeley, Clarke, Eddie Gray and, of course, Norman 'Bites Yer Legs' Hunter.

However, Leeds also had a habit of losing finals. But, to make it your day, you really had to make them second best. And that must have been what Sunderland manager Bob Stokoe said to his troops before they ventured on to the Wembley pitch, prepared to battle Leeds with everything they had. Bobby Kerr, the captain, led from the front. The goal that shocked the football world came after half an hour: Ian Porterfield's name in the history books after latching on to a loose ball and smashing it past David Harvey.

Wearside went mental (although the streets were deserted). They had an hour to keep the lead, and keeper Jim Montgomery proved to be the man for the big occasion. Up to the 65th minute, Monty's handling had been far from perfect, and when Leeds full back Trevor Cherry met a Paul Reaney cross with a bullet header, it seemed that Sunderland's hearts were about to be broken. But Montgomery had other ideas. He twisted in mid-air and parried the header, but the ball fell perfectly for the gifted right foot of Peter Lorimer who lashed it towards the net from six yards. Somehow the Sunderland keeper raised his hands and diverted the ball on to the bar and away to safety.

Leeds had no more to offer. Sunderland became the first Second Division team to win the FA Cup since the 1930s; it was their own last heyday. Stokoe, the master manager, galloped across the hallowed turf and into football heaven.

BOXING World Heavyweight Championship
Muhammad Ali v. George Foreman, Mai 20 Stadium, Kinshasa, Zaire, 30 October 1974

1974

Part Four 1970–1979

Rumble in the Jungle

SAY WHAT you like about Don King, he knows how to promote a fight. And there was no bigger fight and no bigger build-up to a fight than The Rumble in the Jungle. Admit it – it's a good title.

George Foreman against Muhammad Ali was also as good as it got when it came to the Heavyweight Championship of the World. Both men had beaten Joe Frazier: Foreman in a sensational upset, Ali in revenge for his defeat in the Fight of the Century. Foreman, never defeated, was a clear favourite, but not with the people of Zaire. To them, Ali was God. 'Ali, Boom-ay-yeah!' they screamed.

Both boxers spent much of the summer of 1974 in Zaire, getting acclimatised to the tropical heat. A concert, starring James Brown, BB King and Bill Withers amongst others, was organised to accompany the fight. But when Foreman injured his eye during training the fight was delayed. The concert went ahead anyway.

Once they were in the ring Ali proved the critics wrong. From the bell, Foreman was on top, showing the power that had knocked Frazier out. It seemed one-sided. But Ali took whatever Foreman could throw at him (and there was a hell of a lot of it). Introducing us to the 'rope-a-dope', he thrust out right hands, finding Foreman's head. Riled by the tactics and taunts, and exhausted by so much effort for so little reward, Foreman left himself open. After another Ali onslaught in the eighth round, he hit the deck and was counted out by referee Zack Clayton.

This was the Greatest at his greatest – this was truly the Sport of Kings.

A five-punch combination that ended with a left hook brought George Foreman's head into position, a right hand to the face and down he went. Ali knows his work is done.

BOXING World Heavyweight Championship
Muhammad Ali v. Joe Frazier, Araneta Coliseum, Quezon City, Philippines, 1 October 1975

1975

Thriller in Manila

'IT'S GONNA be a thrilla, and a chilla, and a killa, when I get the Gorilla, in Manila'. The Greatest always had a way with words, and Muhammad Ali served up yet another of boxing's greatest ever fights when he took on Smokin' Joe Frazier for the third time in their bitter rivalry to see who was the legitimate heavyweight champion of the world. Round One, the Fight of the Century, had gone to Frazier. Round Two, again in Madison Square Garden, to Ali. Now, after beating Joe Bugner in Malaysia, boxing's world tour had taken Ali to the Philippines, to the dollars of dictator President Marcos.

Frazier really didn't like Ali. Even though the heat and humidity in Manila were ferocious, the fight was furious from the get-go. Neither man wanted to relent. First Ali was all over Frazier, then Frazier on Ali. A trademark left

The third instalment of the trilogy of bouts between Ali and Frazier, both nearing the end of their careers, is regarded as one of the best fights of the 'golden era' of heavyweight boxing.

hook from Frazier in the sixth round would have floored any lesser man. But Ali's skill and his speed around the ring would again prove a decisive factor and he gradually turned the fight around again as Frazier began to tire. In the 11th round Ali started to unload a series of fast combinations, gradually reducing Frazier's face to mush. By the end of the 14th round, he could barely see, let alone defend himself. Trainer Eddie Futch wouldn't let his man take any more.

Ali later said that he was on the point of quitting too; never had he been taken to such extremes. It was as draining, as brutal a bout of boxing as the sport had ever seen. Two heavyweight world champions; only one winner.

The Perfect 10

IN GYMNASTICS, each athlete starts out with a mark of 10 and deductions are made for every mistake. In the compulsory segment of the uneven bars in the team event at the Montreal Olympics, the 14-year-old Nadia Comaneci didn't make any mistakes. For the first time in Olympic history, the judges witnessed a perfect routine and awarded her the maximum 10. Not that the scoreboard registered this incredible score. Since it was regarded as impossible, the board was only programmed for three digits. Nadia scored 1.00. The arena announcer assured everyone this was indeed a perfect 10 but the crowd already knew that and were on their feet. Everyone knew they had witnessed history and a faultless performance. Comaneci went on to repeat the score six additional times in Montreal and took three golds (for the beam, bars and all-round), one silver (floor) and team bronze back to Romania with her, together with the torch that lit the 1976 Olympic flame (she was presented with it, she didn't pinch it) and the affection and admiration of the watching world.

Nadia Comaneci's routine on the uneven bars in Montreal was … faultless – the first time anyone had ever achieved this feat in Olympic gymnastics.

Wilkie Wins Scottish Gold

David Wilkie drinks in the applause after his world record-breaking swim in the 200 metres breaststroke.

THE US men's swimming team won 10 of the 11 available individual gold medals at the 1976 Olympic Games. Quiz question: Who won the other one? Answer: '... and it's Wilkie' as BBC commentator Alan Weeks famously declared when David Wilkie touched home in the 200 metres breaststroke. Wilkie not only won gold but broke the world record by an astonishing 3.1 seconds, 2.16 seconds ahead of his great rival, Olympic champion and holder of the record, American John Hencken, who had beaten him in the 100-metre event. Born in Colombo, Sri Lanka to Scottish parents, he lived on the island for 11 years before moving to Edinburgh. Wilkie headed to Florida to train and study after winning silver in the 200 metres breastroke at the 1972 Olympics in Munich, but he was very much a proud, if laid-back, Scot who became one of the heroes of the British team. His Olympic swimming victory was the first for a British competitor since 1960 and the first for a man for 68 years. Following the Games, Wilkie retired from competition, leaving the public with the indelible image of a winner in goggles, cap – the first top-class swimmer to favour this combination – tiny trunks and 1970s moustache – Britain's very own Mark Spitz.

Hollywood Comes to Formula One

IF THERE was a cooler racing driver, he was in Hollywood. James Hunt might indeed have liked the idea of being Paul Newman, had he not been so thoroughly full of himself. Plus, what he really wanted to be, despite little formal education in his chosen profession, was world champion. And he did it.

The 1976 Formula One season produced countless cliff-hanger moments, not least the crash in Germany which nearly killed Niki Lauda and helped put paid to his ambition to retain his title. Hunt had proved that he could beat Lauda before, even in a Hesketh, but having taken a last-minute berth with McLaren as a replacement for Emerson Fittipaldi, it took the aristocratic Brit some time to work out how to drive it. He was called Hunt the Shunt, after all. But if nothing else, Hunt was bloody-minded and nonchalant about the danger of his sport (at least in public).

A controversial season started badly for him: he was disqualified but later reinstated as the winner of the Spanish Grand Prix; his win at Brands Hatch was wiped out as a result of an accident at the first corner; the fuel he used at Monza was deemed to be too high octane and he was forced to start from the back of the grid. At the halfway point Niki Lauda had a significant points lead in the championship. Things changed in Germany, where Hunt won and Lauda crashed out, missing the next two races. Hunt won again in Holland, then in Canada and the USA. Only Japan remained, in teeming rain. Lauda opted out: he was already a champion, he said, and didn't need to kill himself. Hunt, maniacal, determined, finished fourth despite a puncture and won the title by a point. Ambition achieved. Time for more champagne, preferably with a blonde on each arm.

James Hunt's playboy image, charisma and charm brought a whole new audience to Formula One when he won the sport's world championship in 1976.

Red Rum's Grandstand Finish

Tommy Stack and Red Rum are cheered to the line as they complete one of the Grand National's most popular victories.

TO SOME, Red Rum's first Grand National win over Crisp in 1973 cast him as the villain. But with victory in 1974 and then two consecutive second places, by 1977 Rummy was the public's darling. In a race that featured the National's first female jockey, Charlotte Brew, Red Rum was 9-1 favourite, but in expert opinion this was heart ruling head. After all, he was carrying top weight, at 12 he was surely too old and he was out of form: one win in seven that season. Rummy ignored them.

With Tommy Stack in the saddle, he responded magnificently to the course. When Andy Pandy fell at Becher's on the second circuit, Red Rum was out in front and enjoying himself. Over the last, he flew home to become a legend. The Grand National may have been in the doldrums in terms of attendance then,

but you would never have known it. Peter O'Sullevan summed it up, 'It's hats off and a tremendous reception. You've never heard one like it at Aintree.' Over five years Red Rum had negotiated 150 National fences with only two horses ever leading him home. That was the way it was to stay. The nation's favourite never raced the National again.

Red Rum died on 18 October 1995 and is buried on the finishing line at Aintree. His gravestone contains the words 'His feet would fly, our spirits soar.' As his trainer Ginger McCain said, 'Rather nice, that, isn't it.'

The First Cup Is the Sweetest

IT WAS a turning point in European football. The early 1970s had been a dominant era for German teams, both at national level – winning the 1974 World Cup – and club level, with Bayern Munich having won the European Cup three times in a row. In the Bundesliga though, Borussia Mönchengladbach had won three straight titles, so made for fearsome opposition for Liverpool when the two teams met in Rome with the biggest club prize of all at stake.

Gladbach had won the UEFA Cup in 1975 too, but so had Liverpool in 1976, and Bob Paisley had fashioned a team with unbridled belief. When Terry McDermott gave them the lead, a stadium that was far from full (but mostly red) erupted. But after Allan Simonsen (the future Charlton player no

less) had equalised, then gone close again, and Uli Stielike was only just denied by Ray Clemence, it was hearts-in-mouths time.

Cue one of the greatest moments in the last match of the career of a Liverpool legend, Tommy Smith, whose bullet header from a corner restored the lead. Then Kevin Keegan, in his last game for Liverpool before moving to Germany, was brought down by Berti Vogts, and Phil Neal, as ever, was reliable from the spot and scored off the post. It was the first of five European Cups for Liverpool (as their fans never cease to remind the opposition, especially at Old Trafford) and the first of six consecutive triumphs for English clubs.

Heysel ended that, but the first cup is always the sweetest.

Jimmy Case (left) and Ray Kennedy clutch the European Cup after victory in Rome – at the time the greatest triumph in the club's history.

Tartan Army Invades Wembley

Scottish fans demolish one of the goals at Wembley following their victory. Apparently, the crossbar and pieces of the pitch were smuggled back to Scotland as souvenirs.

ENGLAND 1 Scotland 2. At Wembley. Sweet revenge for the 5-1 drubbing two years previously. A header from Gordon McQueen and a scramble over the line by Kenny Dalglish put the game beyond England before Mick Channon's 88th-minute penalty. The talented Scotland team were on the up, securing a second straight Home Internationals Championship, and would soon be the only British representatives at the 1978 World Cup.

The Scots had turned Wembley into a colourful home match, awash with St Andrew's crosses and Lion Rampants. It should have been a time of celebration and national pride. When Scotland last beat the English at Wembley, in 1967, the fans swarmed on to the pitch in joyous, good-natured exuberance. This time, the atmosphere was altogether different.

To many eyes, this invasion was drink-fuelled destruction. Reports suggested that as many as 70,000 fans had made their way to London, but tales of damage to public transport and unruly behaviour made them far less welcome than the Tartan Army of today would be. And when the Wembley pitch became a sea of Bay City Rollers and Rod Stewart lookalikes, digging up the turf and destroying the goalposts, the death knell began to toll for the Home Internationals and the oldest international fixture in the world.

TENNIS All England Lawn Tennis Championships
Ladies' Singles Final, Virginia Wade v. Betty Stove, Wimbledon, London, 5 July 1977

1977

Part Four 1970–1979

Two Queens at Wimbledon

THE SILVER Jubilee of 1977 saw Britain transformed in celebration of Queen Elizabeth II and her 25 years on the throne. There were street parties, Union Jack bunting and parades up and down the country – there were the Sex Pistols and 'God Save the Queen' too, of course – and after the main Jubilee events in June, Wimbledon started its centenary championships on a wave of patriotism.

The third and fourth seeds in the ladies' singles, Virginia Wade and Sue Barker, carried the hopes of the nation and lived up to expectations, both reaching the semi-finals. Against the odds, the 31-year-old Wade then beat her younger rival and top seed Chris Evert in a titanic three-setter, although Barker was unable to make the final an all-British affair, going down in straight sets. In the final, Wade lost the first set to the tall Dutchwoman Betty Stove, but drew on the fervour of the crowd to launch an amazing recovery and win 4-6, 6-3, 6-1 in a match notable for its tension rather than its quality.

The Queen presented Wade with the famous Venus Rosewater Dish and the Silver Jubilee was crowned with a British victory at Wimbledon. Such scenes have not been seen on Centre Court since.

One of Queen Elizabeth's best Jubilee presents was to see a British winner at Wimbledon. Little did we know then that we'd still be waiting for the next one.

'Duel in the Sun'

SUN-DRENCHED, gladiatorial, skilful, tenacious, mesmerising – Turnberry in 1977 witnessed sport as it should be. By the final round of the 106th Open, there were only two players that mattered. Jack Nicklaus and Tom Watson. Master and apprentice.

For the first three days the two gunslingers stood toe-to-toe shooting identical rounds of 68, 70, 65. Nicklaus was quickest on the draw for day four, surging three ahead by the fourth, only to be pegged back to all square on the eighth. The 12th saw a two-shot swing, Nicklaus firing in a birdie, Watson off-target with a bogey. Reloading, Watson drilled home a 12-foot birdie putt on the 13th.

The defining moment came on the 15th. Watson shot 60 feet from the pin off the green; Nicklaus was sitting within 12 feet. Watson drilled his putt home; Nicklaus missed his. All square again. On 17, Watson nosed ahead when Nicklaus missed from three feet. Had he fired his last salvo? Not quite. Having watched Watson smash a 7-iron to within a couple of feet, Nicklaus cracked a miraculous 8-iron out of heavy rough to manufacture an outside chance of a birdie. From 40 feet, he took it, and Watson's two-footer suddenly looked a lot longer. But he held his nerve, sank the putt and won by one shot. As they walked off, Nicklaus put his arm round the victor, 'I gave it my best shot,' he said. 'But it wasn't good enough.' On any other day, a 66 surely would have been. But then again, this was the Open of Opens.

Jack Nicklaus (left) and Tom Watson, two of golf's supreme competitors, staged the sport's supreme competition at Turnberry in 1977.

Geoff Boycott's Hundredth Hundred

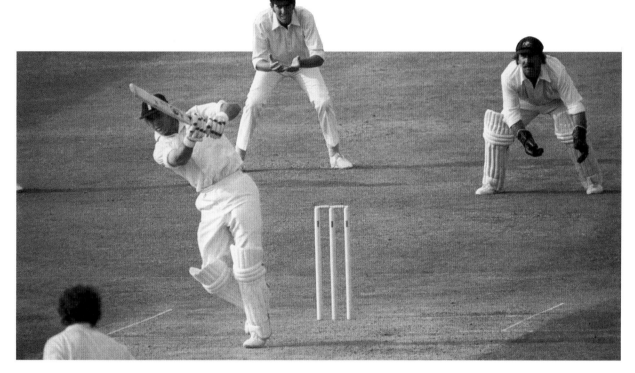

Boycott drives Greg Chappell through mid-on for a boundary that brought up his hundredth hundred during the Fourth Test – becoming the first man to achieve the distinction in a Test match.

YOU HAD to exercise a certain degree of patience when watching Geoffrey Boycott bat. He wouldn't have been ideally suited to Twenty20. For him it was all about technique, and selecting your shots. In that manner, he was the consummate opener, and he certainly chose his moment to score his hundredth hundred in first-class cricket.

The venue, of course, was Headingley. The opposition, of course, was Australia. Boycott had only recently returned to the England team, managing to enrage the whole of Nottinghamshire by running out Derek Randall at Trent Bridge. But England were 2-0 up in the series. It was the Fourth Test and a perfect summer's day.

Boycott lost his opening partner, captain Mike Brearley, in the first over, but from then on (one dropped Rodney Marsh chance and another hearty caught-behind appeal aside) it was sweetness of timing and lightness of touch. The century came with an on-drive off the bowling of Greg Chappell. A roar rang round the ground. Champagne (and Tetley's) was brought on to the pitch as Yorkshire's hero was engulfed by fans, losing his cap in the process. No helmet for Boycs. He even bowled with his cap on.

It was a sublime moment and was followed by an Ashes victory.

Cambridge Get that Sinking Feeling

IN ALL sports, training is important – for fitness, to assess ability and, crucially, to learn. In 1978, in training for the annual Boat Race, the Oxford crew sank. As a result, they made sure to have splashboards fitted for the actual race. The Cambridge crew did not. Oxford had won handsomely the previous year, and although they were favourites once again, the 1978 Cambridge boat knew the chasm in class and experience had narrowed. Oxford were favourites, but Cambridge had a chance. Passing under Hammersmith Bridge, Oxford has a four-second lead – significant, but not insurmountable. Up to then the weather had been calm and the rowing fast. After Hammersmith it was anything but. Out of the blue a wind picked up, chopping the calm surface of the Thames into debilitating

It was all going so well … until rough water whipped up by a 'howling sou-wester' took over and the Cambridge crew's chance of victory went down with their boat.

waves. Rounding the Surrey bend, Oxford had stretched their lead, but as both boats made to traverse The Crossing, to the relative safety of the Middlesex bank, Cambridge seemed to be closing the gap. Who knows what would have happened … if they had fitted those splashboards. They battled bravely to stay with Oxford, but it was an impossible contest. The river was always going to win. Under Barnes Bridge, less than a mile from the finish line, the boat gave up the fight, stern first, as the Cambridge cox, followed by his teammates, began to disappear from sight. That's what sport's all about.

The Archie Gemmill Show

IN 1978 Ally McLeod's army was on the march to Argentina and, according to the manager, Scotland were going to return with at least a medal.

The campaign began well against Peru, with a Joe Jordan goal after 14 minutes. That proved to be a mistake. The unfancied Peruvians woke up. Two thunderbolts from Hector Cubillas left keeper Alan Rough stranded, helping Peru to a 3-1 victory. Next up was Iran. Football giants they were not, but Scotland failed to score on their own, handed a 1-1 draw courtesy of an own goal.

To qualify for the next stage, Scotland had to beat the Dutch by three clear goals. No chance? Without the intervention of the crossbar and the ref's decision to disallow a Kenny Dalglish 'goal', Scotland could have been two up before Robbie Rensenbrink netted a disputed penalty. Dalglish scored before half-time to give hope, and for the first 25 minutes of the second half it was the Archie Gemmill show. A penalty made it 2-1 and then, in the 23rd minute, on the corner of the Dutch box, he beat one, beat two, slipped through a third and lifted the ball over the sprawling Dutch keeper for 3-1. One of the tournament's greatest goals had put Scotland in dreamland … for three minutes. Johnny Rep blasted in from 30 yards for the Dutch and the impossible proved … well, impossible.

He's on his way … Archie Gemmill is a study in concentration as he carves his way through the Dutch defence and into the Scottish football history books.

Arsenal Win 'Three Minute' Final

The agony and the ecstasy – Alan Sunderland (in yellow) turns away in triumph after scoring the winner for Arsenal in the last minute of the FA Cup final.

SCORING A last-minute goal to win the FA Cup is the ultimate schoolboy dream. For Alan Sunderland, that dream came true and capped one of the most memorable of FA Cup finals. Well, at least the last three minutes were, and that is what you really remember from 1979.

Arsenal were 2-0 up with Liam Brady the star of the show, pulling the strings in midfield, his left foot dictating the play. Brian Talbot got the first, then Brady's inch-perfect chip was met by a textbook Frank Stapleton header before half-time. Arsenal were cruising, but Manchester United were not done. With three minutes left on the clock Gordon McQueen stuck out a leg in a penalty-box melee to make it 2-1. On 88 minutes Sammy McIlroy twisted, turned, shot and the ball dribbled over the line for an incredible equaliser. The United end went wild.

From the kick-off, Brady again picked up possession, surged forward and passed left to Graham Rix. He looped the cross to the far post, where Sunderland slid in – 3-2 and bedlam among the Arsenal fans this time. Blink and you could have missed it, and a lot of United fans did, still celebrating McIlroy's goal. Yet it was a dream final for all who were there: a sunny day, on a perfect Wembley pitch – just as it is meant to be.

Forest's Fairy Tale Triumph

Trevor Francis heads Forest's European Cup winner against Malmö, in a triumph masterminded by Brian Clough and Peter Taylor.

JOHN ROBERTSON'S run down the left, beating two defenders, and cross, deep to the far post. The £1 million man Trevor Francis (making his European debut) arching his back to get his head on the ball, past Malmö keeper Jan Möller and into the net. Nottingham Forest, European champions. Unbelievable.

It could never happen again: a small-town club winning promotion to the top division, then winning the league championship, then becoming champions of Europe in the space of two years. And the following year lifting the trophy again, against Hamburg in Madrid. Nottingham Forest, the only club to sit at the pinnacle of European football more times than it has its own domestic competition.

For fans appalled by the rich list that the Champions League became, the European Cup was good old-fashioned knockout football. Maybe the Swedes weren't the strongest of opposition ('a boring team', in Brian Clough's words), but Forest had beaten Liverpool in the first round, with Garry Birtles setting them on their path to glory. As always, Clough and Peter Taylor had prepared their team immaculately. The fact that Forest won 1-0 was down to a brilliant team effort: Larry Lloyd and Kenny Burns at the back with captain John McGovern dictating play in the middle. And if it was at times a little dull, as Clough said: 'We still won, so who cares?'

Seve Wins it His Way

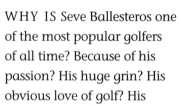

WHY IS Seve Ballesteros one of the most popular golfers of all time? Because of his passion? His huge grin? His obvious love of golf? His sublime skill? It is for all these reasons, but also because of the way he approached the game, like a marauding conquistador – dashing, flamboyant, dangerous and dazzling. And never was this more apparent than when Seve secured his first Major at Royal Lytham & St Annes to become the youngest winner of the Open in the 20th century.

Trailing Hale Irwin by two strokes going into the final round, he produced a display of golf that mesmerised the crowd and announced a new superstar. Irwin faded quickly but throughout that fourth round Seve had to jostle for top spot on the leader board with Ben Crenshaw and Rodger Davis, with the maestro Jack Nicklaus lurking ominously in the background. In cold and blustery conditions and engaging in close combat with such luminaries of the game, how did Seve mount his challenge? Playing safe and steady? No, that was never his style.

Instead, as the pressure built over the closing holes, he opened up and let fly, blasting his last seven tee-shots wildly, visiting the crowd from where he manufactured a par, a car park from where he conjured a birdie and his 15th greenside bunker of the tournament to steal another crucial par. This was golf the Seve way and it was a joy to watch … and to cap it all, he won.

Seve Ballesteros celebrates another outrageous shot on his way to winning the Open in 1979, the first of his five Major victories.

The Sheene–Roberts Classic

BY 1979, Barry Sheene had ceded the dominance he had enjoyed in becoming double world champion to the American Kenny Roberts, whose Yamaha had outstripped the British rider's Suzuki in every department in 1978. If anything, though, that made for greater drama – Sheene had just about waltzed to his titles in 1976 and 1977. The stage was set for a classic race at the British Grand Prix at Silverstone in August 1979 – it turned out to be one of the most exciting races in motorcycle history.

Roberts made a slow start, down in fifth place at the end of the first lap, and almost crashing before passing Virginio Ferrari, his sole remaining rival for the 500cc title that year.

Kenny Roberts on a Yamaha YZR500 leads Barry Sheene on his Suzuki GT500 during the thrilling British Grand Prix at Silverstone in August 1979.

Dutchman Wil Hartog was also in the running, but not for long. This would be a two-man race.

For most of the 28 laps, Roberts and Sheene toyed with each other, took turns in spurring each other on, visibly gesturing at each other, and all at 150mph. It was almost a game, although both men knew enough about crashes not to take it too lightly. On the final lap, and there was nothing between them, Sheene's last valiant attempt at overtaking came up short, by a wheel. It was thrilling; it was Sheene all over. He never came closer to winning the British Grand Prix.

Part Five
1980 | 1989

Hammers Beat Gunners

Goalscorer Trevor Brooking (left) and Frank Lampard celebrate as unsung Second Division West Ham deservedly beat Arsenal at Wembley.

AS FA Cup finals go, it was probably not the best – just the one goal, a bit scrappy – but try telling that to the West Ham faithful. The Hammers' win over Arsenal in 1980 was a classic triumph of the underdog, and is still the last time a team from outside the top flight lifted the famous trophy. West Ham were fully deserving of their victory. Led from the back by the imperious Billy Bonds, a local hero if ever there was one, and with Frank Lampard, Trevor Brooking and Alan Devonshire classy in midfield, John Lyall's team simply ran and ran, resisting everything Arsenal could throw at them.

After Brooking's early headed goal, stooping to convert Stuart Pearson's shot, Phil Parkes was hardly tested at all. That was testament to how good West Ham were on the day. Of course it should really have been 2-0, because of the game's most memorable – and scandalous – moment. Who could forget 17-year-old Paul Allen, the youngest player to appear in an FA Cup final, through on Pat Jennings' goal, cynically hacked down by Willie Young, and even worse, the defender staying on the pitch? It still leaves a sour taste in the mouth in the East End of London.

TENNIS All England Lawn Tennis Championships
Men's Singles Final, Bjorn Borg v. John McEnroe, Wimbledon, London, 6 July 1980

1980

Part Five 1980–1989

Borg Takes Five

IN SOME contests, there just are no neutrals. And in 1980, at the Wimbledon men's singles final, it was either Borg or McEnroe. It was a simple split, between two absolute opposites. Cool, Swedish, right-handed Borg, going for his fifth straight Wimbledon title. Fiery, American, left-handed McEnroe, at 21 in his first final.

McEnroe's antics had already alienated him from the conservative tennis establishment, notably during his semi-final against Jimmy Connors. The media and public picked up on this prejudice and he was actually booed when he made his way on to Centre Court. No matter – McEnroe breezed to a 6-1 first set and it seemed as though the brash pretender would end the Borg era. But Borg bounced back, and then there was the fourth set. The tie-break.

Five match points saved by McEnroe. Twenty minutes of exhilarating action, swinging first one way then the other. Both Borg and McEnroe fans had hearts in mouths. The American prevailed 18-16, but Borg again showed amazing powers of recovery and consistency in the fifth. At the end it was Borg, victorious, who sank to his knees, less in celebration than pure emotional exhaustion. McEnroe was cheered to the rafters too – a hero now to the crowd for the heart, soul and guts he had displayed in this classic match – and his time would come the following year. Borg and McEnroe had served up a treat. Was this the best ever Wimbledon final?

It was a familiar picture in the late 1970s – Bjorn Borg with the Wimbledon trophy – but rarely had he been pushed so hard as he was by in 1980 John McEnroe during 3 hours and 53 minutes of gripping tennis.

1980

Britain Dominates Olympic Track

ALTHOUGH THE build-up to the 1980 Olympics was dominated by news of the boycott of the Games by 60 countries, including the USA, in protest at the USSR's invasion of Afghanistan, when they eventually got underway British interest was intense, particularly on the track.

'Come on Allan!' Above the cheers in the Lenin Stadium as the men's 100 metres final

(Above) Allan 'Wipper' Wells (foreground) dips to take 100 metres gold from Cuba's Silvio Leonard (in lane one).

burst into just over ten seconds of action, one voice could be picked out – Allan Wells's wife and trainer, Margot, screaming encouragement. The starting line-up may not have included the Americans Stanley Floyd and Mel Lattany but you can only beat those who are there.

Wells did so in an electrifying race, the result of which was not clear until the stadium's large-screen slow-motion review confirmed that the Scot had dipped to the line inches ahead of

Cuba's Silvio Leonard. Watching on the track, Wells leapt and span in balletic motion when he realised victory was his.

Thirty years on, he is the last white man to win the Olympic gold, the last even to make the final. For doubters of Wells's inclusion in the list of great world sprinters, in the same Games he was pipped to a second gold in the 200 metres by 0.02 of a second; two weeks after the Olympics he dispatched Floyd and Lattany in a World Cup race in Koblenz; and in 1982 he roared past a regulation-sized Ben Johnson to take the 100 metres title at the Brisbane Commonwealth Games. Oh, and his middle name was Wipper!

The public perception was that Steve Ovett was the intense one, Seb Coe the more carefree; Ovett the hard worker, making himself more than the sum of his parts, Coe just naturally gifted. No wonder Ovett was beaming on top of the podium in Moscow. Not just an Olympic gold medal, but Coe annihilated, left gasping for air, destroyed by Ovett's blinding speed, politely accepting silver. And this was the 800 metres, with the 1500 metres still to come. Yet that was when Coe, to everyone's astonishment, turned Ovett over, inflicting a first

The two runners were like chalk and cheese.

defeat on the Brighton man at that distance for three years, digging so deep that he left his rival with just a bronze.

Both races were riveting. The media had stoked the feud between the two runners and it wasn't hard: they were like chalk and cheese. It was really the start of a saga that would see world middle-distance records broken and swapped like so many toys. There is little doubt that Coe and Ovett spurred each other on to become the finest athletes of their generation.

(Top) Steve Ovett smiles broadly during the medal ceremony for the 800 metres; Seb Coe has a grimmer expression on his face that shows how much he needed his revenge in the 1500 metres (right).

Aldaniti Beats the Odds

'A FAIRY TALE outcome' was how Peter O'Sullevan described Aldaniti's victory in the 1981 Grand National. He was spot on. First off, the chestnut horse surely wasn't cut out for the rigours of Aintree. Rejected by his mother at birth, Aldaniti suffered a string of leg injuries and breakdowns that should have ruled him out of racing altogether. But trainer Josh Gifford had faith.

As for Bob Champion, working in a profession that's all about odds, he shouldn't really have been at the tape of the 1981 National either. Diagnosed with testicular cancer in 1979, he was given a 40 per cent chance of survival, and that was with taking experimental chemotherapy drugs. He opted for the pioneering approach, deciding he didn't want to die; he wanted to ride again.

Despite a bad start, Aldaniti and jockey Bob Champion ran the race of their lives in the Grand National at Aintree in 1981, holding on to beat the favourite, Spartan Missile, by four lengths.

Suffering terribly at the hands of the drugs that were saving his life, Champion pulled through but the fairy tale was almost over before it began. Landing over the first, Aldaniti seemed to buckle, but somehow his legs held. Champion clung on and as they jumped the last they were two lengths clear, with Spartan Missile closing.

It was down to a strength-sapping charge for the line. The heart said Aldaniti; the head said Spartan Missile. But that was ignoring one crucial fact: the courage of the partnership. Together Aldaniti and Champion wanted the prize more and held off the challenge, eventually pulling away to an astonishing victory. Against all the odds.

Ricky Villa's Redemption

THE GOAL has been replayed countless times. The greatest in an FA Cup final? Perhaps. It was named Goal of the Century. But has there ever been another goal, especially a goal in Wembley's showpiece event, that was so utterly full of redemption?

Ricky Villa was dire when Spurs and Manchester City first contested the 1981 FA Cup final on 9 May, the 2-2 draw requiring a replay five days later. He was hauled off by Keith Burkinshaw and replaced by Garry Brooke. He cut a disconsolate figure as he walked around the cinder track, disgusted, furious and in tears. Villa hadn't wanted to leave Argentina in the first place. He was quite happy at home in the countryside, but Ossie Ardiles had persuaded him – and Burkinshaw – that they were better off making the move as a pair. Villa scored a brilliant goal on his debut, against Nottingham Forest in the league, but hadn't done a great deal since. It was all about Ossie and his dream.

Under ten minutes into the replay, Villa smashed a loose ball home, with all the venom imaginable. Spurs then had to come from behind, drawing level through Garth Crooks. And then came the immortal moment: 'Villa … And still Ricky Villa!' in the words of John Motson, as Villa slalomed inside and outside the City defenders, drew keeper Corrigan, dummied to shoot and then slotted the ball home. It was the first goal that gave Villa the confidence to take on half the City side. The warmth of the subsequent embrace between Ossie and Ricky, the two brilliant Argentinians who were taken into the hearts of Tottenham fans and who revolutionised English football, was beautiful to behold.

Ricky Villa slides the ball past City keeper Joe Corrigan to provide a fitting climax to what had become a classic FA Cup final.

Shergar: Triumph Then Tragedy

HAVING FALTERED over the previous year, Shergar's three-year-old season in 1981 was almost perfect. Five wins, one loss. Ridden by a 19-year-old Walter Swinburn, trained by Michael Stoute and owned by the Aga Khan, Shergar won the Sandown Classic Trial by 10 lengths, the Chester Vase by 12 and the Epsom Derby by 10. He won both the Irish Derby (under Lester Piggott, with Swinburn suspended) and the King George VI and Queen Elizabeth Stakes by four. Only in the St Leger did he fail to perform.

When the name Shergar is mentioned, it should be the Derby win above all other achievements that immediately springs to mind. Coming round Tattenham Corner into the home straight, the odds-on favourite with the distinguishing white blaze on his face moved up equine gears the others did not know existed. He thundered past Riberetto and Silver Season, dropping to a canter as he passed the post to win by the longest winning margin in the race's 226-year history.

That should be the image that is conjured up. However, instead that image is of TV coverage of policemen, press conferences, helicopter searches and, ultimately, of despair. The £10 million syndicate-owned wonder horse was kidnapped for ransom 18 months after his Derby triumph. He was never seen again.

The Derby field rounds Tattenham Corner with Shergar (front left) poised to strike for home – his speed so great that he opened up a gap of ten lengths on the home straight.

1981

Mac's Back

AFTER 41 straight wins at Wimbledon, Bjorn Borg met John McEnroe for the second consecutive year in the men's singles final. The last man to beat the Swede on the courts of SW19 was Arthur Ashe in 1975 – on American Independence Day the tennis gods were always going to favour the boy from New York City. So it proved.

This was the championships of 'You cannot be serious' fame, a phrase spat out in McEnroe's first round match against Tom Gullikson; but during the final, McEnroe behaved impeccably. Borg started the better, taking the first set 6-4. McEnroe's first serve then began to take effect, putting Borg on the back foot, reducing his ability to pass and giving the serve-and-volleyer room to manoeuvre. The serve proved to be McEnroe's key weapon, saving 13 break points of the 15 he faced. Critically, he held it together in the second and third set tie-breaks, which he won 7-1 and 7-4. As his final, match-winning volley dropped inside the baseline, McEnroe dropped briefly to his knees then, perhaps to avoid copying Borg's victory pose over the past five years, quickly raised himself to shake hands at the net.

The pair would meet only once more in a Grand Slam final, two months later at Flushing Meadows. There, McEnroe would again win in four sets after losing the first. Before the presentation too place, the 25-year-old Borg had decided to walk away from tennis for ever.

John McEnroe hit the heights in 1981: he beat the unbeatable Bjorn Borg at Wimbledon and took over his world No. 1 title.

Willis's Bowling; Botham's Ashes

Ian Botham hooks Geoff Lawson to the long leg boundary in his match-winning innings of 149 not out – one of the finest examples of power hitting ever seen in Test cricket in England.

AT THE end of the third day, England followed-on 227 runs behind. Gooch was out for a duck, with Brearley and Gower soon to follow. Another Ashes defeat seemed inevitable. What followed was quite extraordinary. Ian Botham hauled England back into the game with a sensational 149 not out in the second innings in which he flayed the Aussie bowlers – but they still needed only 130 to win the match. Then Bob Willis took over.

A ball speared into Trevor Chappell's neck looped behind to Bob Taylor. Australia captain Kim Hughes and Graham Yallop were both out for ducks. Then after Chris Old had bowled Allan Border, Willis swept up the tail. Ray Bright was the last man out, stumps splayed. Willis had the 8 for 43 figures that would define his career, and he sprinted off as a trademark 1980s pitch invasion began.

Not to be outdone, in the next Test at Edgbaston with the Australians again set for victory, needing only 37 runs with five wickets remaining, Botham got busy again, this time with the ball. His bowling was pitch perfect, pinpoint accurate, unplayable. Rod Marsh bowled middle stump from around the wicket. Ray Bright lbw next ball; Botham pumped his fists in the air. Then, after Dennis Lillee had been caught behind by Bob Taylor, two more Aussies were clean bowled and Botham hared down the pitch to collect his stump. The sun shone, the crowd roared, Botham was God. Of course, England went on to win the Ashes.

Erica Roe Delivers Pep Talk

BILL BEAUMONT'S England were 6-3 up at half-time in their match against Australia. The players were huddled together on the pitch to receive their captain's words of wisdom on how to finish the Wallabies off, when all thoughts of strategy and game plan went out of the window, thanks to a bookseller from Hampshire. Resplendent in jeans, boots, a neck scarf and nothing else except a cigarette hanging out of her mouth, 'busty Erica Roe'™ ran into rugby history as the first female streaker at Twickenham. Giving the fans a *Generation Game* style twirl, to ensure all sides of the ground had the opportunity to enjoy the moment, she – with her similarly attired and often-forgotten friend Sarah Bennett – was soon surrounded by stewards and led away, modesty being poorly preserved by first a Union Jack and secondly a policeman's helmet.

The *Rothmans Rugby Union Yearbook* described this incident in style, explaining that proceedings were interrupted 'when a lady named Erica erupted onto the field like a galleon in full sail but minus her spinnakers'. Play eventually resumed and England went on to win 15-11, with both Australian tries being scored, appropriately, by Brendan Moon. Quite why Erica chose a freezing day in January is anyone's guess.

A policeman does his best to cover up Erica Roe's credentials; quite what England mascot Ken Bailey (in the Union Jack hat) is doing on the pitch is anyone's guess.

The People's Champion Swaggers to Victory

Ray Reardon (left) and Alex Higgins shake hands before the 1982 World Snooker final. Ray Reardon's nickname was Dracula – can't think why.

AT THE beginning of the 1980s, Alex Higgins was at the height of his flamboyant powers. Having won the snooker World Championship at his first attempt, in 1972, he brought sex appeal, excitement and glamour to a sport previously stuck in dimly lit clubs. Higgins didn't always toe the line, but there was a certain charm then to his erratic behaviour that appealed hugely to the growing television audience for snooker.

The 1982 semi-final against Jimmy White was a classic, with Higgins constructing one of the game's greatest breaks under pressure in the penultimate frame. Ray Reardon, his conqueror six years previously, was Higgins' opponent in a tense final, the crucial moment coming at 17-15 with Higgins requiring one more frame to win. Reardon broke and potted the cue ball. The reds

were spread but Higgins only had one pot on, long to the top-left pocket. Miss it and Reardon would probably clean up. He executed the shot to perfection and went on to make 135 and take the title.

In a display of raw emotion, the Hurricane called his wife Lynn and daughter Lauren to join him for the presentation. With tears streaming, he hugged and kissed them while clutching the trophy. The fights, the divorce, the drunken moments, the incidents of domestic violence, the bans, the assaults on officials, the cancer and his sad, lonely death were all to come. For that moment, he truly was the People's Champion.

Torvill and Dean's Golden *Bolero*

WE SHOULDN'T really be any good at sports on ice, should we? Some would say that figure skating is not really a sport at all. But in the wake of Olympic gold medals for John Curry in 1976 and Robin Cousins four years later, along came a couple to capture the hearts of a nation in 1984.

Jayne Torvill and Christopher Dean were just everywhere. The Nottingham couple (Were they? Weren't they?) were already multiple gold-medal winners, British, European and World ice dancing champions, but with their *Bolero* routine in the Sarajevo Winter Olympics, they reached a new pinnacle. A British television audience of 24 million (yes, that's 24 million!) watched Torvill and Dean slide and sway in perfect harmony to their finale, stretched out together on the ice, to a standing ovation from the crowd.

When the marks came up for artistic impression, there was a collective gasp: nine perfect sixes, across the board. Though hardly an occasion for the red-blooded male sports fan, it was sporting perfection. There were flowers, dancing – it even happened on Valentine's Day! – and no one can deny that it was deeply memorable.

Nottingham's finest figure skaters prove the impossible – that you can be British and be good at sports on ice.

Grobbelaar's Wobbly Knees

WHO KNOWS what was going through Bruce Grobbelaar's mind when the European Cup final between Liverpool and Roma went to penalties? He was, to put it mildly, unpredictable. It might have gone something like this …

'The boss has said he won't blame me if I don't save any, but I should try to put them off. Just standing there for the first one didn't achieve much. If only Stevie Nicol had put his away. Come on Phil. You've scored already in the match … and again! Good man. 1-1. This place is buzzing. Cameras everywhere. I'll give them a nice smile, look super-confident and relaxed even though my stomach's a mess … How about if I take a bite out of the net before Conti takes his kick? That should confuse him. Here it comes … miles over!

'Big Graeme's up next. No bother: 2-1 to Liverpool. I'll play it straight this time … that was a mistake. He sent me totally the wrong way. 2-2. Come on Rushy … yes! 3-2. If I can just do something now to put doubt in Graziani's mind, but what? I am having enough trouble walking, my legs feel like jelly. Hold on …

'If I'm tired, he must be dead on his feet. After all, the European Cup has never gone to penalties before. Best I remind him just how knackered he is. A touch of the old spaghetti legs should do the trick. Here he comes … bye bye! It's down to you now Alan. Yes! Champions for the fourth time! Mamma mia!'

Kennedy may have scored the decisive kick in 1984, but on Roma turf, Grobbelaar was the real hero.

Roma's Francesco Graziani blasts the ball over the bar to hand the penalty shoot-out advantage to Liverpool. Whether it was Grobbelaar's antics that put him off or not … it was an inspired piece of play-acting.

John Barnes Scores that Goal Against Brazil

SCORING YOUR first goal for England is always going to be a magical, breakthrough moment. For John Barnes, then aged 20, it offered us a brief glimpse of football from another planet.

The scintillating Watford winger had only made his international debut the previous year, coming on for club teammate Luther Blissett in a 0-0 draw against Northern Ireland, and even if this was hardly a vintage England team – they should have been at the European Championships, not in South America – it was at least potentially exciting, with Stoke's Mark Chamberlain on the other flank. But Barnes' wonder goal against Brazil, just before half-time at the Maracana, was the ultimate solo effort.

John Barnes celebrates doing to Brazil what they'd been doing to everyone else since the late 1950s.

Gliding past players as if they weren't there, Barnes had the ball on a string and, unbelievably, put England 1-0 up. From one of the winger's crosses, Mark Hateley went on to seal a famous and landmark win (admittedly, England haven't played in Brazil since, and Bryan Robson should have made it three) and a new star was born. Yet it never quite happened for him in an England shirt, despite 79 caps, and ten more goals. If only Bobby Robson had brought him on earlier against Argentina in 1986. But for this one, extra special moment, John Barnes really was that good.

Budd's Shame and Daley's Glory

Budd stayed ahead but began to fade as derision filled the LA Coliseum ...

ZOLA BUDD arrived in the UK in March 1984 amid considerable controversy. Born in South Africa, a country banned from international sport because of apartheid, she was the unofficial world record holder at 5,000 metres. Thanks to a British grandfather, she was quickly granted citizenship. Five months later, this slight, 18-year-old, 5-foot 2-inch, barefoot runner in a British vest had tens of thousands of people booing her.

The first women's 3,000 metres race in Olympic history was billed as a showdown between Budd and America's sweetheart, world champion Mary Decker. No one seemed to notice the fastest time that year had been set by Romanian Maricica Puica. To have any chance of winning, Budd needed to stretch the field, and with just over three laps to go she moved ahead.

Going ... going ... gone, the clash before the fall as Budd (151) and Decker come together. Watching the incident: Puica (316) and Wendy Sly (175) went on to win gold and silver respectively.

Budd and Decker made contact, stumbled, but settled. They clashed again but stayed up. Five paces later, the race was over for both of them.

Decker tumbled to the track and, with tears flowing, was unable to finish. Budd stayed ahead but began to fade as derision filled the LA Coliseum stadium. With 250 metres to go, Britain still had hopes of gold. Wendy Sly had kept pace with Puica but was unable to respond to the Romanian's finishing burst, settling for silver. Budd faded to seventh, though she claimed afterwards that she slowed down because she could not stand the possibility of collecting a medal in front of such a hostile crowd.

He led from the very first event, the 100 metres …

Throughout the 1980s it was nip and tuck. First one was in the ascendancy, then the other. The contest between the rivals captivated the imagination and brought athletics' most challenging discipline to a wide audience. Whenever battle once again commenced over ten gruelling events, numerous column inches were invested in analysing the enthralling sporting question of the decade. The issue? Was Daley Thompson a loveable rogue or too confident for his own good? You either saw the swearing as he was announced BBC Sports Personality of the Year, the whistling of the national anthem on the Olympic podium, his wearing of a T-shirt bearing the legend 'Is the world's second greatest athlete gay?' and his insinuation that he would like to have a baby with Princess Anne, as bringing colour and fun to

Whatever you want … Daley does it all: running, jumping, throwing and vaulting, winning gold with a new Olympic points record.

a sport that usually produced single-minded, dull individuals; or you regarded such antics as the physical manifestation of perhaps a more complex character.

What was never in doubt was his athletic ability, proven time and time again when it mattered most. Constantly pushed hard by the other great decathlete of the era, Jürgen Hingsen, the moustachioed Thompson won every title going, culminating in his brilliant performance at the LA Olympics when he led from the very first event, the 100 metres, to successfully defend his crown and re-take the world record from his German rival. A complex character perhaps, but definitely a phenomenal sportsman.

Taylor's Late Finish

An unlikely sports hero, Dennis Taylor won the world snooker crown when the sport was at the peak of its popularity.

PEOPLE UNDER the age of 30 may not believe it, but there was a time when snooker was the most popular sport on television. The audience figure – of 18.5 million, on BBC2, after midnight – for the epic 1985 World Championship final remains a record for BBC2 and for any channel post midnight. Northern Irishman Dennis Taylor was very much the underdog against 'Interesting' Steve Davis, the three-time and defending champion and by far the best player in the world at the time.

It seemed that no one could combat the Romford player's steady potting and precise safety play, and when Davis won all seven frames of the opening session, it became even more likely that this would be one of the shortest finals on record. But Taylor bounced back by the end of play on Saturday to trail only 9-7 and remained resilient, even when Davis went 17-15 ahead in the Sunday evening session. Taylor drew level and, incredibly, the 35th and deciding frame went down to the final black.

The tension among the crowd at the Crucible Theatre was unbearable, and seemed to get to Davis as he overcut a pot. In a match lasting a total of 14 hours and 50 minutes, Taylor sank the last ball at 12.19 a.m. and became world champion. There were a lot of tired people at work that Monday morning.

The Bradford Fire

THE LAST game of the 1984-85 season should have been a celebration of Bradford's promotion to the Second Division. But of the 11,076 supporters who attended Valley Parade that day, 56 would never return home. An additional 265 people suffered injuries. A discarded cigarette or match ignited the decades of rubbish accumulated under the main stand, built in 1909 – the renovation of which was due to begin a few days later. The deadly combination of a highly flammable structure, a roof covered in bitumen and asphalt and windy conditions meant that within four minutes of the first sighting of smoke, the whole structure was engulfed. Valley Parade did not have high security fences, common in football stadiums in the 1980s as an attempt to curb hooliganism, which gave

Towards the end of the first half smoke was spotted in the old stand and the fire brigade was called. Evacuations began immediately but within four minutes the whole stand was engulfed in flames.

those fans who made their way forward on to the pitch a route to safety. Those who headed back to the entrance gates found most of them locked and the turnstiles inoperable. It was in this area that most of the fatalities occurred.

The subsequent Popplewell Inquiry made a number of safety recommendations for UK sports grounds, including no new wooden stands and proper health and safety training for stewards. The Bradford Disaster Appeal raised over £3.5 million, part of which funded the burns unit at Bradford Royal Infirmary, which played a crucial part in the aftermath of the horrific tragedy.

1985

The Heysel Tragedy

IN FOOTBALL terms, there was a lot at stake on the night of the 30th European Cup final. Liverpool were looking to ensure they did not end up without a trophy for the first time in ten years. They were also on the brink of capturing Europe's premier competition for the fifth time, in what was Joe Fagan's final match in charge. Their opponents, Juventus, were aiming for a first European Cup victory, and to become the only club to have won all three major European trophies.

Approximately one hour before kick-off, none of that mattered any longer. The rival fans had been segregated, but between one of the Liverpool areas and what was meant to be a neutral section, there was only a narrow gap and a flimsy fence. Around 7 p.m., some Liverpool supporters made a charge through the fence towards the neutral zone, which contained mainly Juventus fans. Fighting broke

out and, as the Italians peeled away, their way was blocked by a perimeter wall, which some started to climb as the crush became deadly. The mass and rush of people proved too much for the structure and it collapsed, many falling 40 feet from the back of the exposed terracing. Thirty-nine people lost their lives, mainly Italians. Hundreds were injured.

Despite the situation, the authorities decided that abandoning the game would risk inciting further trouble, and went ahead with it. Juventus won 1-0 with a Michel Platini penalty. But the score was an irrelevance. English clubs were subsequently banned from European competition for five years, with Liverpool facing an additional year's expulsion.

Ground staff and police examine the terraces of the already dilapidated Heysel Stadium in Brussels after the tragic events of 29 May 1985.

110

Barry Does the Fighting

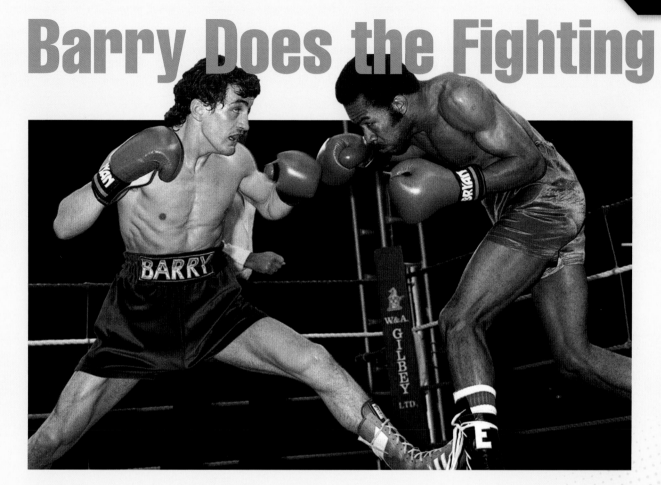

'BA-REEE, BA-REEE!' As the final notes of Pat McGuigan's emotional rendition of 'Danny Boy' drifted into the night sky, 27,000 fans inside Loftus Road chanted his son's name as he stood facing the defending WBA featherweight champion of the world, Eusebio Pedroza from Panama.

QPR's home ground had been transported for the night to Belfast, where McGuigan was a national hero across the sectarian divide. As a Catholic married to a Protestant, he represented an inspiring figure of religious unity. 'Let Barry do the fighting' was the slogan and at Loftus Road he certainly did. Following the bizarre and unsettling appearance of a dwarf dressed as a leprechaun dancing around the ring sprinkling fairy dust, the Clones Cyclone focused on the task at hand, and it was considerable. Pedroza had been champion for seven years, with 19

Barry McGuigan had the night of his life in front of an ecstatic crowd at Loftus Road in London when he beat world featherweight champion Eusebio Pedroza.

successful defences under his belt. McGuigan set out to sap his strength and he did, staying lively and landing significant hits.

The key moment came in the seventh round when the Irishman floored the champion with a right–left combination. From there on, there was only going to be one outcome. At the final bell, McGuigan was the unanimous winner. Amid scenes of euphoric celebration and pandemonium, McGuigan demonstrated his true quality, dedicating his victory to Young Ali, the Nigerian fighter he had knocked out three years previously, who had fallen into a coma and never recovered. Barry McGuigan was a worthy champion of the world.

The Young Pretender Becomes King

Boris Becker, a 17-year-old unseeded outsider when the tournament began, raises his arms in victory to rapturous applause from the Centre Court crowd.

IN 1984 Boris Becker left SW19 in a wheelchair, having suffered a nasty injury in his third round match against Bill Scanlon. In 1985, he left as the first unseeded, the first German and the youngest ever (at 17 years, 227 days) Wimbledon men's singles champion. Boom Boom had arrived and it was glorious and exciting to watch.

Although all but unknown to the Wimbledon public, Becker was in fact ranked 20th in the world and that year had won the Queen's Club title. On the way to the final, Becker had faced Joakim Nystrom serving for the match in the second round, and had to save two match points against Tim Mayotte in the last 16. Henri Leconte and Anders Jarryd were dispatched without such pressured moments.

In the final, played in glorious sunshine, he faced Kevin Curren, runner-up in the Australian Open the previous year and conqueror of McEnroe and Connors. Throughout the match Becker offered up his full repertoire – big serves, spectacular diving volleys, a never-say-die attitude and considerable aggression and athleticism. It was too much for Curren and Becker triumphed 6-3, 6-7, 7-6, 6-4. When his final serve sped past Curren, he raised his arms, turned his face to the sky and the crowd rose to acclaim a new star.

Death of Jock Stein

THE 12,000 Scottish fans streaming out of Ninian Park on the evening of 10 September 1985 should have been heading to the bars and clubs of Cardiff in jubilant mood. They had just watched their team secure a 1-1 draw against Wales that ensured them a World Cup play-off encounter with Australia, but the result didn't matter. Not to them, and not to the Welsh supporters and team either when news spread of what had occurred at the end of this highly charged match.

The atmosphere was febrile. Scotland had equalised from the penalty spot only ten minutes from time, and the benches were surrounded by photographers and other stadium staff ready for the final whistle. The referee blew for a free kick. Jock Stein thought that was it and stood up from his seat. Seconds later the Scottish manager, football legend and all-round gentleman collapsed in the dugout. He was carried immediately up the tunnel by the medical staff but died moments later in the treatment room. Stein was 62 years old. One of the true greats of the game had gone. He never knew he had guided his team to within striking distance of qualification for the 1986 World Cup, and never felt the pride when they took that chance. That role was taken by his assistant on the night, one Alex Ferguson.

Jock Stein's last decision as a football manager had been to replace Gordon Strachan with Davie Cooper in the 61st minute. Cooper scored Scotland's crucial penalty.

Jock Stein (left) watches the final match of his illustrious career in the company of his assistant Alex Ferguson.

The Empire Strikes Back

DECKED OUT in his standard-issue red European jumper, with matching pencil tucked behind his ear, Sam Torrance knew that one last great shot would all but wrench the Ryder Cup out of the tight US grasp of the past 28 years. Having been three down through the tenth, and all square after the 17th, he had just witnessed US Open champion Andy North send his drive to a watery death.

As his second shot soared over the lake protecting the 18th and settled 20 feet from the pin, Torrance raised both hands to salute the cheers from the gallery, greeting the hugs of his captain Tony Jacklin with his customary broad grin. The only thing now between Torrance and golfing immortality was ... his teammate Howard Clark, who had a putt on the 17th to secure the winning point. Clark missed and it was down to Torrance. He had three for it, but only needed one. Pure magic.

As the delirious Belfry crowd cheered, and players sprayed champagne from the clubhouse, Big Sam hoisted Jacklin on to his shoulders. 'For he's a jolly good fellow' rang out from players and spectators alike. There was a delightful simplicity to the scene, which was a million miles away from the football-style chants of 'Yourup!' heard at more recent events. The celebrations lasted long into the night. With the likes of Torrance and Ian Woosnam in the team, they would.

(Left) Sam Torrance in familiar pose practises his celebrations after a birdie on the ninth, and does a jig of delight with playing partner Howard Clark (below) after his birdie on the 15th.

Malcolm Marshall Gets Up Gatting's Nose

YOU REALLY did not want to face West Indian fast bowlers in the 1980s. If the first one didn't get you out, the next one would. They were relentless, vicious, with pace and bounce that sent grown men back to the pavilion quaking – and in the case of Mike Gatting in Jamaica in 1986, with a seriously damaged face.

It was the first one-day international (ODI) of a pretty disastrous tour. The West Indies were at their awesome best: Greenidge and Haynes to open, Viv Richards the skipper, and a pace attack including Joel Garner, Courtney Walsh and Malcolm Marshall. Ouch. It was actually Patrick Patterson, on his home pitch and making his debut, who brought Gatting to the crease after seeing off Tim Robinson and David Gower for ducks.

Gatting reached 10 and then took on one Marshall bouncer too many. His nose shattered, leaving shards of bone embedded in the ball, which – to make a bad day worse – careered on to the stumps. Allan Lamb walked (when he hadn't made contact with the ball) rather than take further punishment. Gatting was soon on his way back to Heathrow. 'Where did it hit you?' a reporter asked.

Despite winning the second ODI, England lost the rest and were then 'Blackwashed' in the Test series that followed. Quite simply they were annihilated by one of the most devastating attacks in world sport.

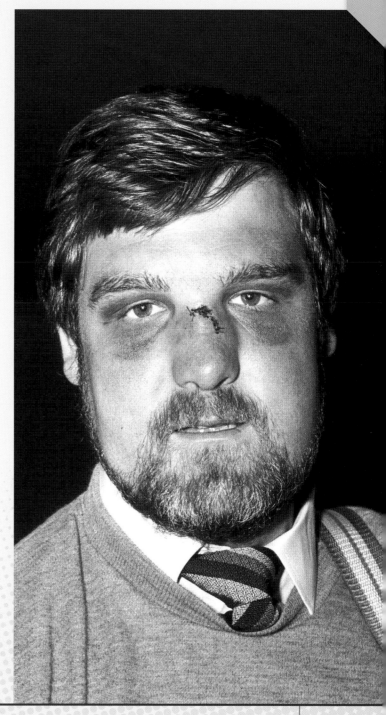

Mike Gatting arrives home from the Caribbean bearing the scars made by Malcolm Marshall's fearsome bouncer.

Lineker's Efforts Not Quite Good Enough

(Above) Lineker boots in one of his three against Poland; (opposite) Maradona helps it home with his hand. Lucky he scored a worthy winner.

ENGLAND WERE in desperate need of a lift or they would be heading home from the Mexico World Cup before it had really begun. An inglorious start to the campaign had seen defeat to Portugal and a hapless 0-0 draw with Morocco. Something special was required and in 36 glorious minutes, Gary Lineker provided it with a breathtaking display of the goalscorer's art, made all the more impressive as his left wrist was fractured and bandaged.

Often dubbed the 'poacher's hat-trick', this does a disservice to the quality of the finishing. The first, after eight minutes, was made at Goodison. Initially linking well with Peter Beardsley, Lineker fed Trevor Steven on the edge of the Polish box; he in turn moved the ball on to Gary Stevens. As Stevens drilled the ball across, Lineker evaded his marker and tucked it away. Five minutes later, Beardsley was again involved, cleverly finding Steve Hodge on the left. His first-time ball was met perfectly by the right foot of an on-rushing Lineker. To be fair, the third was a poacher's gift, when Poland's goalkeeper Mlynarczyk fumbled a corner straight into Lineker's lap, for him to complete only the second English hat-trick in the World Cup finals (the first is quite well known) with his left foot.

Lineker went on to get his hands on the Golden Boot award as top scorer with six goals. Unfortunately, Maradona got his hand on the ball and sent England home in the quarter-final.

A little bit with the head of Maradona, a little bit with the hand of God.

'A little bit with the head of Maradona, a little bit with the hand of God.' Give him credit; it was a very clever post-match sound bite. And while this was the moment that would burn in England's hearts for eternity (and be celebrated north of the border), the rest of the world remembers Maradona's second goal in that World Cup quarter-final, the Goal of the Century, together with the fact that Argentina's No. 10 played quite breathtaking football all game long (and even had time to fix a corner flag).

Of course 'La Mano de Dios' was unfair. But it went deeper than that. This was a reaction to Alf Ramsey calling the Argentinian players 'animals' in 1966, to the deaths of young Argentinians in the Falklands. Well, at least with the benefit of hindsight. At the time, it was simply an instinctive footballing reaction, like the defender's hand that snakes out to stop a goal on the line.

The referee should have spotted it, as the Ireland players were at pains to point out after another famous sleight of hand in 2010. It was a foul, which Maradona got away with, from a horrible slice (for the second time in the game) by Steve Hodge. Despite Gary Lineker's efforts in Mexico '86, England weren't quite good enough.

The Unlikely Hero

IN THE list of unlikely heroes, the name of Keith Houchen must figure quite highly. Yet thanks to one fabulous diving header in an FA Cup final his name will live on for football eternity.

A classic case of the journeyman footballer – his career had taken him to Hartlepool, Orient, York and Scunthorpe before he joined Coventry – Houchen was hardly a prolific scorer at any of his clubs. But he became the talisman of the Sky Blues' Cup run, with four goals: the winner at Old Trafford against Manchester United in the fourth round, two at Sheffield Wednesday in the quarter-final and one in the semi-final against Leeds United.

Few favoured Coventry at Wembley, especially when Clive Allen gave Spurs the lead (his 49th goal of the season!), but it became an enthralling, ding-dong battle. Dave Bennett's opportunistic equaliser. Spurs in front again. It would be Gary Mabbutt's own goal in extra time that won it for Coventry, but for some reason, in retrospect it seems as though it was Houchen. Dave Bennett's beautiful, curving cross – Houchen launching himself into the air, and planting the ball past Ray Clemence to force the additional 30 minutes. Sublime. We all love diving headers, don't we? But can a club like Coventry ever win the FA Cup again?

Keith Houchen scored some important FA Cup goals in his career: a penalty for York as they beat Arsenal in the fourth round in January 1985; the winner as Coventry beat Manchester United at Old Trafford, also in the fourth round, in January 1987; and this cracker against Spurs in the final three months later.

TENNIS All England Lawn Tennis Championships
Men's Singles Final, Pat Cash v. Ivan Lendl, Wimbledon, London, 5 July 1987

1987

Part Five 1980–1989

Cash Clambers into the History Books

It's up, up and away as 'superman' Pat Cash reaches the VIP stand to celebrate his Wimbledon men's singles title with his family.

IT TAKES quite something to become a popular Australian in England, but years before Shane Warne enchanted the world of cricket, another wild man from Down Under, Pat Cash, had his day in the sun. And how he reaped it.

Cash was just unstoppable at Wimbledon in 1987. With his trademark black and white checked headband and muscular athleticism, he bounded from court to court and round to round, losing just one set throughout the tournament, to Michiel Schapers in the third round. Guy Forget, the masterful Frenchman; Mats Wilander; Jimmy Connors, at 34 enjoying an Indian Summer, were all dispatched in straight sets. Ivan Lendl provided little more opposition in the final and, once a first set tie-break had been negotiated, the Czech again crumbled on the big stage.

So after barely breaking sweat, it was time for the Aussie with the 1980s rock-star looks to perform a party piece. Cash clambering into the Centre Court VIP stands to embrace his father (Pat Cash Senior, of course), his family and his coach was one of those classic Wimbledon moments. Was it spontaneous? Who cared? He was the first to do what has become commonplace, and for that, and victory, he has his place in history.

Faldo: Par for the Course

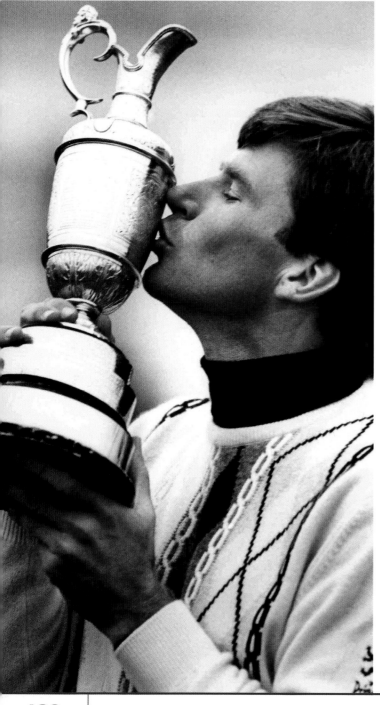

WE ALL like our sport to be packed with excitement, but sometimes it is the steady hand that wins the day. And you can't get much more steady than the remarkable final round that won Nick Faldo his first Open Championship in 1987.

The weather at Muirfield had been miserable – misty, wet, cold and windy – all week and leading contenders like Tom Watson and Bernhard Langer had dropped by the wayside. By the final round, it was a battle between the Australian Rodger Davis, the tall American Paul Azinger and Faldo, with the hopes of a nation on his shoulders. Could he follow Sandy Lyle's groundbreaking success of 1985? He could, and he did it with 18 straight pars: perfect golf, you could say.

Azinger could claim to have lost it – he bogeyed his final two holes for a round of 73 and a one-shot deficit – but it was Faldo's tactics and oh-so-solid execution of them that won the day. He would go on to win the Open again in 1990 and 1992, but there's no time like your first time, especially the day after your birthday. Especially in that brilliant, brilliantly dull, fashion.

Often in contention but never the prizewinner, 'Fold-o', as he was known to some, put it all right at Muirfield in 1987 when he won the first of his six career Majors.

Europe Beat the USA at their Own Game

WE ALL know that the Americans are a patriotic bunch. Nothing is therefore sweeter than beating them at what they think is their own game, at their place and – to cap it all – for the first time in 60 long years of trying.

Europe had come close to snatching an away victory at Palm Beach in 1983. Four years on, and with that precious jinx-ending win at the Belfry under their belts, Tony Jacklin's men came to Ohio with confidence brimming. Crucially, they also had a certain José María Olazábal in their ranks, and this was the start of a partnership with compatriot Seve Ballesteros that would become pure Ryder Cup gold.

By Saturday lunchtime, the Spanish pair, in fetching salmon pink, had posted three points out of three with brilliant, if unbelievably tense and narrow, victories over whomsoever Jack Nicklaus threw at them. Europe's other big guns – notably Ian Woosnam and Bernhard Langer – chipped in with exceptional shots at decisive moments, and a five-point lead was taken into the final day. This was surely ours.

Never write off the Americans, though, and a storming comeback threatened to wreck all the good work. Yet through the debris of defeat after defeat, unsung heroes emerged. Wins for Howard Clark and Eamonn Darcy, who drove Ben Crenshaw so apoplectic that he snapped his putter in two. It was left to Seve – of course – to seal the win. Olazábal danced. Jacklin cried. Unbelievable celebrations, all the way back to Heathrow.

Seve (left) and captain Tony Jacklin look both surprised and delighted as Europe win the Ryder Cup on American soil for the first time in the tournament's history.

Gatt Loses It

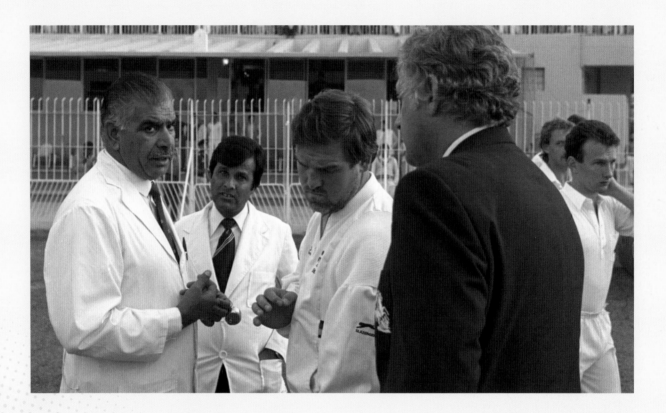

Mike Gatting turns away in disgust as England team manager Peter Lush (in suit) tries to talk some sense into umpire Rana (left). Result: an escalating row that had to be sorted out by the Foreign Office.

ENGLAND HAVE had some genteel cricket captains down the years – Colin Cowdrey, Mike Brearley, even Andrew Strauss – but Mike Gatting was definitely not one of them. Gatting's three years as skipper were certainly eventful, and included an Ashes victory in Australia (one of the few times that has happened, need we be reminded, and his only Test Match victories too). In the middle of all this was the incident that had the press screaming 'It's just not cricket!' with self-righteous indignation.

As we know, it doesn't take a lot to spark conflict between Pakistan and England, but in Faisalabad in December 1987, Gatt really lost it. Pakistani spinner Abdul Qadir had routed England in the First Test, and once again, on the second day of the Second Test all the decisions

had been going the hosts' way. Umpire Shakoor Rana had already annoyed the England players by wearing a Pakistan sweater and cap and enough became more than enough when he accused Gatting of cheating by moving a fielder (David Capel) behind his back. It was preposterous, and the finger-wagging and shouting led to an international incident, a lost day's play (which cost England the game), but, in the end, neutral umpires. For that, we should be relieved. And you couldn't help but stick up for Gatting.

Eddie the Eagle Soars

THE WORDS 'British ski jumping hero' had never been used before, and will probably never be used again. That title, and that of British No. 1 and British record holder, can only belong to one man: Michael Edwards. The plasterer from Cheltenham, rather better known as Eddie the Eagle, stole the show at the 1988 Winter Olympics.

Eddie finished last, as is well known, but what can sometimes be forgotten is that he was dead serious about his sport (and as he joked, if he hadn't been, he'd probably be dead). An accomplished downhill skier, he suffered like many of our Winter Olympians from lack of funding, and switched disciplines to achieve his dream.

He trained with the Finns before the Games – they would win all three ski jumping gold medals on offer in Calgary – and he was as dedicated as any sportsman. Amongst numerous problems, broken bindings meant that Britain's champion had just the single practice jump before the big event. And he jumped, not with impeccable style, but four times, successfully, to a record distance of 73.5 metres on the Big Hill, becoming a genuine Olympic hero. A figure of fun to many, but still Britain's best at his chosen sport.

Michael Edwards overcame tremendous odds – poor eyesight, no equipment, no sponsorship and little practice – to become the only Briton ever to compete in the Olympic ski jumping competition.

Sandy Lyle
Wins Masters

IT IS one of the most famous shots in golf. Sandy Lyle out of the fairway bunker on the 18th in the final round of the 1988 Masters. If he strikes it sweetly, he has a chance of becoming the first British player to wear the Green Jacket. But the omens are not in his favour. Lyle had won the Greater Greensboro Open days before, and no player had triumphed at Augusta after winning the previous week since Sam Snead in 1949.

Then there was Amen Corner (the 11th, 12th and 13th holes). Would that prey on his mind? Bogey, double bogey, par, turned a three-shot lead into a one-shot deficit. Lyle had rallied, and by the 18th was tied with Mark Calcavecchia, but who knew what doubts might be lurking in the genial Scot's mind? His one-iron off the tee

It's somewhat appropriate that Sandy Lyle's shot out of the bunker at the 18th should win him the Masters and be remembered as one of the most famous in golfing history.

had been true enough, but had skipped left towards the bunker. Calcavecchia, in the group in front, made par, leaving Lyle a birdie to win. The moment of truth. Feet planted firmly in the white sand, he whips a seven-iron, and scampers out of the bunker to see his destiny.

Initially subdued, the crowd begins to erupt. Landing past the pin, Lyle's ball had at first hesitated, then slowly, slowly spun back towards the hole. It left him one putt of 15 feet to become Masters champion. He made it, performing a passable jig of delight before the relief swept over him.

The Underdog has its Day

IT WAS, of course, one of the greatest upsets in FA Cup history, especially as it happened in a final. Liverpool were football royalty, blessed with the best players in the land: Hansen, Beardsley, Barnes, Aldridge, McMahon, with the great Kenny Dalglish as manager. Wimbledon were not just underdogs, but were perceived to play like them – snarling, long-ball merchants embodied in the uncompromising figure of Vinnie Jones.

People would not accept the fact that the Dons had finished sixth and seventh in their first two seasons in the top flight, that first Dave Bassett and then Bobby Gould, with Don Howe the most perceptive of assistants, had moulded the south London club into a formidable outfit. They were a good team, with absolutely nothing to lose. Dangerous opponents.

The 1988 FA Cup final was admittedly a poor game, but what an astonishing result. From Jones's crunching tackle on McMahon three minutes in, Wimbledon just would not allow Liverpool to flow, and they would always pose a danger from set-pieces. Lawrie Sanchez flicks in Dennis Wise's free-kick. You what? Dave Beasant saves John Aldridge's penalty. Excuse me? Unbelievable, but also meticulously planned, and in the end, the Wimbledon keeper lifted the cup. Every underdog has its day.

All eyes are on the ball as Lawrie Sanchez (far left) heads in Dennis Wise's free-kick to secure one of the most unlikely FA Cup final results in history.

Van Basten: Dutch Master of Europe

IN BETWEEN the (relative) highs of the World Cups of 1986 and Italia '90, the European Championships of 1988 saw an abject England performance. Three games, three defeats, back home. The rot set in with Ray Houghton's early goal for the Republic of Ireland, before Bobby Robson's team were crushed 3-1 by both the Netherlands and the USSR, who would go on to contest the final. Disappointing as the tournament seemed from an English perspective, it was absolutely lit up by the Dutch, with their sea of orange fans, and by one man in particular. The Netherlands were strong in all departments – the Koeman brothers, Frank Rijkaard, Ruud Gullit in his moustache and dreadlocks phase – but Marco van Basten was off the scale. Van Basten's incredible angled volley in the final sealed the deal, but his hat-trick against

England set the Dutch on their way. It was classic centre forward play – close control, with Gullit the orchestrator, then deadly poaching.

The Netherlands were the neutrals' favourites, and beating the West Germans in the last minute of the semi-final with another sublime Van Basten finish certainly helped. Of course, brilliant as Dutch football has been down the decades, this remains their only major tournament success.

(Above) Dutch striker Marco van Basten scores the second of his three goals as the Netherlands beat a disappointing England 3-1 at the Rheinstadion in Düsseldorf.

Hockey Hits the Headlines

Sean Kerly (on the ground) shoots, well, 'lunges at the ball' as he remembers it, to score his hat-trick and fire Great Britain into the final at the expense of the much fancied Australians.

A PIPE-SMOKING goalkeeper, a trainee hairdresser, a newsagent, a teacher, a doctor, a former marketing manager – not everyday Olympians in the modern era, yet in many ways they represented what the Games should stand for. Here were members of a team who had put careers on hold and made personal sacrifices to chase a dream. They caught it on a hot afternoon in Seoul and became heroes to millions. Perhaps most surprising of all, they did it playing hockey.

It was no flash in the pan. Four years earlier, ten members of the 16-man squad won bronze in Los Angeles, but Team GB started their Seoul campaign inauspiciously. They threw away a two-goal lead against their Korean hosts, drawing 2-2 and, following a win against Canada, lost their third match to West Germany. Victories over the USSR and India secured a semi-final against Australia. Again pegged back to 2-2, having been 2-0 up, Sean Kerly completed a sensational hat-trick right at the death to put GB into the final.

A wonderful solo effort by Imran Sherwani, a penalty corner by Kerly and a second from Sherwani put paid to the West Germans this time, despite a 69th-minute consolation goal. At the final whistle, the British players threw their hands up, leapt with joy and hugged each other. So did the rest of the country.

127

Jocky Holds his Nerve

'JOCKY ON the oche!' The phrase is sure to make any darts fan smile a – perhaps toothless – grin. Jocky Wilson is one of the most popular characters ever to take up the arrows and in 1989 he competed with his great rival Eric Bristow for the World Darts Championship.

This was the first tournament in the 'clean' era, with players banned from drinking during matches, so Jocky took to sucking wine gums as he sought his second world title. Wilson blasted Bristow away from the outset, streaking to a 5-0 lead at the break, requiring one more set to win. But Bristow had fight and guile in spades: 5-0 became 5-3, with Wilson snatching at his darts. Nerves began to play a part in the proceedings. At two legs apiece, Bristow missed a double to

One of the world's most unlikely sportsmen, Jocky Wilson played a big part in darts' rise up the ladder of sporting popularity during the late 1980s and early 1990s.

win the leg and on 104, Wilson had three darts to become champion. Thud, treble 18. Thud, 14. That meant 36 required. The camera zoomed in on double 18. Thud. Nothing. The camera panned out, finding the dart nestled just above double top. The Scotsman had miscounted.

Bristow took the leg and the set: 5-4. But in the tenth set, Wilson held himself together and hit double 10 to take the title. He sank to his knees, then hugged Bristow in recognition of this classic and sporting contest. People may question whether darts is actually a sport. They wouldn't if they'd watched this incredible drama.

Bruno Proves He's the Real Deal

Frank Bruno shows that he's got what it takes as he trades punches in the opening round of his first fight with the fearsome Mike Tyson.

'KNOW WHAT I mean, 'Arry?' It was Frank Bruno's catchphrase, honed from hundreds of interviews with the late, great commentator Harry Carpenter. For some, Bruno became a figure of fun, not helped by his frequent appearances in panto. Yet back in 1989, Bruno was at his prime as a fighter and in awesome shape when he went to Las Vegas to take on 'Iron' Mike Tyson for the undisputed heavyweight championship of the world.

There was still only one champ then, and Tyson was fearsome: 22, six years younger than Bruno, undefeated, raging but controlled. His fights were often over in seconds. Two thousand British fans had followed Bruno to Vegas: the atmosphere was electric and the bout began

with a blaze of punches from both men. Bruno took an early count, but most importantly he took the fight to Tyson and by the end of round one was rocking the American. It was sensational. Could Frank really beat Tyson?

The answer was no – he was stopped in round five – but even if Bruno did become champion in the end, beating Oliver McCall before losing to Tyson again in 1996, it was that first fight that proved that he was the real deal: brave, strong and proud.

The Hillsborough Disaster

DISASTER STRUCK the world of football on 15 April 1989. The FA Cup semi-final between Liverpool and Nottingham Forest was to be played at Hillsborough in Sheffield, with Kenny Dalglish's Liverpool team, the reigning league champions, strong favourites to advance to the final. But football soon took a back seat as the terrible events of the day unfolded.

The Leppings Lane end of the ground was already packed but thousands were still outside as the game kicked off, and as the congestion and frustration mounted, more fans were directed by the police into the back of the stand. They surged forward to get a better view of the action, crushing those people already in place who were unable to move as perimeter fencing had been put in place to prevent hooligans invading the pitch. In the desperate crush, 96 Liverpool fans lost their

The day after the tragic events at Hillsborough the gates of Anfield were opened to allow the hundreds of supporters gathered at the Shankly Gates to lay scarves and flowers on the goal in front of the Kop in tribute to the victims.

lives and hundreds more were injured as they tried to escape. In the confusion, the match was abandoned after six minutes, but the full extent of the tragedy would only become known later.

It was football's third major disaster in four years, following the Bradford fire and the Heysel Stadium tragedy, and left the reputation of Britain's national sport at an all-time low.

The Taylor Report that followed the Hillsborough disaster saw long-lasting changes to the game, such as the removal of fences at the front of terraces and the introduction of all-seater stadiums.

The 96 victims are mourned to this day, but their families still seek justice for what happened.

Thomas's Last-Minute Glory

IT CAN easily be forgotten that Arsenal's championship victory at Anfield came just six weeks after Hillsborough. The Michael Thomas goal that gave the Gunners the title on goals scored, in the final minute of the final game of the season against their title rivals, seems completely divorced from the horrible reality of the earlier tragedy. It is perhaps etched on the faces of Kenny Dalglish and the Liverpool team as they realise that the title has been snatched away. But perhaps the reason that we remember the incredible finale – Thomas had already blown a perfect chance to put the ball past Bruce Grobbelaar; John Barnes had only to keep the ball in the corner and the whistle would have blown – is the fact that football can produce such drama, and that it will go on even after the worst of times.

The Kop, magnificently, applauded Arsenal's achievement that night as the Gunners collected the trophy on the pitch, and their title success in 1989 is a story like no other. Memories of the game are strong: George Graham's odd, but ultimately successful decision to pick three centre-backs at Anfield, controversy surrounding Alan Smith's opening goal from Nigel Winterburn's free-kick, the excruciating time added on at the end. Then Lukic, to Dixon, to Smith, to Thomas, and the celebration – an expression of pure, disbelieving joy.

A goal so famous that it caused a moment's silence across north London as the ball made its way from Michael Thomas's boot to the back of the Liverpool net. What followed was … pandemonium.

Part Six
1990 | 1999

Scotland Feast on the Spoils

Scotland's Derek Turnbull (third from left) shows the commitment needed to win rugby's Grand Slam as he wrests the ball from England's Peter Winterbottom.

AGAINST A backdrop of Poll Tax demonstrations and rising anti-English sentiment, the 1990 Calcutta Cup match at Murrayfield was always going to be highly charged, for the fans at least. For the players it was all about rugby spoils in a Grand Slam, winner-takes-all encounter.

The feeling within Scotland was that the English press had shown arrogance; claiming their team only had to turn up to win. Any such claims of complacency within the England camp, however, were misguided. Players of the stature of Dooley, Ackford, Probyn and Winterbottom don't know the meaning of the word. But when Scotland's captain, David Sole, walked his team on to the pitch at an ominous death-march pace, even they must have felt the impact, as the atmosphere flew off the scale.

England had played with flair in their previous three matches, but an early break by Finlay Calder, followed by the dynamic drive that sent England backwards and led to Craig Chalmers' first penalty, exemplified Scottish commitment. At half-time the Scots were 9-4 up, and within moments of the restart Bill McLaren was describing the destruction of English hopes. 'Pick up by Jeffrey. Jeffrey to Armstrong. Armstrong nicely out to Gavin Hastings. Gavin Hastings with the kick through. On goes Stanger. Stanger could be there first. It's a try!'

A penalty brought England within six points, but for all their battering of the Scottish defence, Sole's men stood firm to win only the third Grand Slam in their history and send England home with nothing but memories of what might have been.

Platt's Flash of Inspiration

THE FIRST knockout stage of Italia '90: England versus Belgium. After an eventful 90 minutes, in which the Belgians hit the woodwork, Peter Shilton pulled off some crucial saves and John Barnes had a goal disallowed for offside, the two teams were heading for penalties after 29 minutes of extra time had failed to produce a breakthrough. Paul Gascoigne picked up the ball in his own half and made a surge forward, beating two defenders but blocked by the third. Free-kick. Gascoigne took it. Lurking along the line of defenders in the box was substitute David Platt, brought on for Steve McMahon. As the free-kick floated in, Platt watched its flight, pirouetted and, as the ball drifted over his right shoulder, hooked it across a static Preud'homme and into the Belgian net. England were on their way to a quarter-final with Cameroon and the players piled on top of Platt in celebration.

Gazza's immense value to England's chances of lifting the trophy was clear from his dominating performance, but three minutes before the end of normal time he had picked up a yellow card for what he protested was his first foul of the game. Noticing Gazza's dismay at the decision, the Belgian No. 2, Eric Gerets, put a generous consoling arm around his shoulders, almost as if he had a premonition of the consequences of the moment.

Last-minute goals are always thrilling, but in the World Cup and with a quarter-final place at stake, they are like gold dust. David Platt (leaning back) is clearly pleased with his.

Gazza's Tears

THE 1990 World Cup was memorable for many things but no image is as redolent of the tournament as Gazza's tears. Bobby Robson's England faced up to old foes Germany in the semi-final in Turin, brimming with confidence and inspired by the genius of young midfielder Paul Gascoigne.

After going 1-0 down early in the second half, Gascoigne's Spurs teammate Gary Lineker equalised for England with ten minutes remaining to force extra time. But Gascoigne, having already received a yellow card during England's 1-0 victory over Belgium in the second round, was then booked again for a foul on Thomas

Getting booked, out of the final, unable to take a penalty, losing the match … it was all too much for Gazza. Mind you, the England fans were pretty upset too – so near, yet so far.

Berthold, meaning that he would be suspended for the World Cup final if England won the match. Lineker tried to console Gascoigne but the midfielder was distraught.

The game went to penalties. Gascoigne felt unable to take one, and after Chris Waddle blazed his spot-kick over the bar, the Germans were victorious, and England had failed once again. A phenomenon known as Gazzamania was born, however, with football – thanks to Gazza's tears – reaching out to a whole new audience.

Navratilova Crowned Queen of Wimbledon

THE 1990 Wimbledon ladies' singles final may not have been the most thrilling of all time, with Martina Navratilova brushing aside Zina Garrison, but its significance rests in the fact that it marked the beginning of the end of a period of dominance over the championships that had never been seen before and probably never will be again.

Navratilova always had a love affair with Wimbledon, but it is fair to say that when she won her first title, way back in 1978, the SW19 crowd did not share that affection. The reason? Navratilova was taking the crown of Queen of Wimbledon from the darling of the court, Chris Evert – the once fairytale-fiancée of Jimmy Connors when they both captured the title in 1974, and the then girlfriend of our own John Lloyd.

Navratilova repeated the offence in 1979, but as the years progressed and her incredible ability and love of the tournament shone through, Wimbledon embraced her in an eternal hug of affection. She retained her title in 1982 and from there on appeared in nine consecutive finals through to 1990, winning seven of them. When she eventually waved an emotional goodbye to the famous grass courts in 2006, she had collected a total of 17 Wimbledon titles, including, incredibly, the mixed doubles in 2003 at the age of almost 47. Navratilova wears her crown as the Queen of Wimbledon very well.

Not one to hide her feelings – Martina Navratilova wept with joy after beating the American Zina Garrison to take her ninth Wimbledon singles crown.

Gooch Scores a Triple Nelson

WITH HIS trademark white helmet, high backlift and rigorous approach to the game, Graham Gooch was the most distinctive of cricketers. He was also one of the most distinguished, and his greatest innings came as England captain in the First Test against India at Lord's in 1990. A triple century and – even better for the conspiracy theorists – out for a Triple Nelson.

India could hardly have known what was coming when they put the hosts into bat, especially after Mike Atherton was first man out, bowled by Kapil Dev for just 8. By the end of the first day, though, Gooch was on an astounding 194 not out with Allan Lamb chipping in with a ton. An extraordinary second day saw the Essex opener reach his landmark figure plus a century for Robin Smith.

The stats don't make good reading for the Indians: Gooch was in for 10 hours and 28 minutes, faced 485 balls, hitting 43 fours and three sixes before being bowled by Prabhakar.

India, astonishingly, avoided the follow-on when Kapil Dev hit four straight sixes off Eddie Hemmings, but that only brought Gooch to the crease again. Another majestic innings of 123 (nice and neat once more) in a double century opening partnership with Atherton put the game beyond reach. Gooch's 456 runs remains a world record for a batsman in a Test match. On that honours board at the home of cricket, he stands mighty proud.

Great batsmen consistently fail to score 456 runs in a Test series. Good ones often don't score that many in a Test career. Graham Gooch did it in one Test match. Unsurprisingly, it remains a Test match record.

Back in the Saddle

RETIREMENT HAD not been easy for Lester Piggott, following a career that included nine Derby wins and many more Classics. The master horseman lived and breathed racing and found it difficult to settle to life as a trainer after he packed away his silks in 1985. Then came his conviction for tax fraud and a year and a day spent at Her Majesty's pleasure.

Released in October 1988, the only place for him to go was surely back into the saddle. After gentle persuasion from trainer Vincent O'Brien, Piggott agreed, and on 11 October 1990 he was granted his riding licence, at the age of 54. It was in the USA that Piggott rode into town two weeks later and stole the show.

The Breeders' Cup Mile was a $1 million, Grade 1 race and, following an injury to O'Brien's regular jockey John Reid, Piggott was given the ride on the favourite, Royal Academy. He was the perfect choice, his experience and steely nerves ideally suited to holding the horse back until the optimum moment to let him fly. Last coming out of the stalls, Piggott settled towards the rear, waiting patiently. On the home turn, he made his move. Inside the final furlong, he still had two in front of him. On the line, there were none. Royal Academy won by half a head. Welcome back Lester.

Born to ride: Lester Piggott returned to racing in 1990 following a spell in prison. He finally retired in 1995 with an incredible 4,493 career wins.

Boxing's Bitterest Rivalry

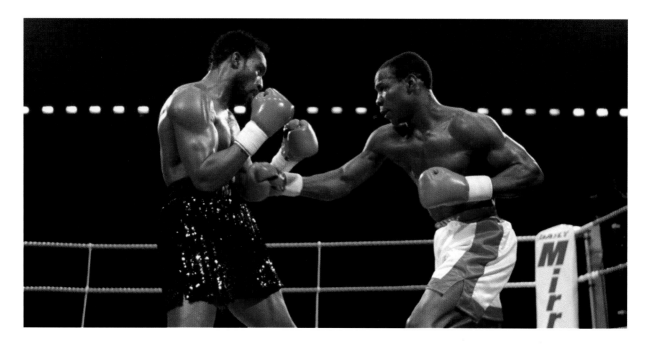

Best of enemies: Nigel Benn (left) and Chris Eubank brought their rivalry into the ring in one of the most dramatic fights ever seen in a British boxing ring.

BRITISH BOXING has had its share of bitter rivalries, but few can match the feelings Nigel Benn and Chris Eubank had for each other. It was definitely mutual. Of course, Eubank brought it on with his preening showmanship, his 'Simply the Best' tag, but he could get away with it because, well, on his day he was. And when Benn, the 'Dark Destroyer', took him on for the WBO World Championship in 1990, it was one of the most intense fights ever seen.

The pair stalked each other from the bell, dripping with venom as well as sweat, and the clash went one way then the other. Eubank blooded in the fourth round. Benn's left eye shut by the fifth. They were still level by the eighth, when Eubank crashed to the canvas. A slip, he claimed. Again in the next, Benn on top,

exhausted yet getting in the body punches. But Eubank, with a fury that belied all the posing between rounds, unleashed a flurry of punches that stopped the fight. Incredible.

That was as good as it got for both men. The rematch, at Old Trafford three years later, at super middleweight, was another classic, but a draw. The ultimate anti-climax. Both fighters lived through tragedies to their opponents: Michael Watson and Gerald McClellan, both suffering appalling long-lasting injuries. When both boxers lost to Steve Collins, the end was in sight. But together they produced one of the sport's best ever nights.

Langer Gets the 'Yips'

THE 'YIPS' are the putting dread of every golfer. When they strike, you can take remedial action, but there is no permanent cure, as Bernhard Langer found out throughout his illustrious career. Especially at the Ryder Cup.

At Kiawah Island, Langer was employing an unconventional left-hand-down-the-shaft-right-hand-securing-handle-to-left-forearm grip which had helped secure him a point with Colin Montgomerie in the Saturday afternoon four-ball. On the Sunday, the singles went down to the wire, with Langer–Irwin the final match. With two to play, Langer was one down and required a victory to level the scores at 14-14, which would leave the trophy in Europe's hands. This was not something the US players or fans could countenance, given the fervently patriotic atmosphere that pervaded the tournament, following the First Gulf War.

In blustery conditions and with spectators and players ringing the 17th green, sitting on the fringe and even in the bunker, Irwin faced a tricky 6-inch putt to halve the hole and secure victory. He missed and Langer kept his nerve from 5 inches. From the 18th tee, Langer was in the driving seat. Irwin was in the crowd, then off the green, followed by a poor chip and a putt that was left not quite dead. Langer, for his part, was left with a 6-foot par putt to win the precious point required. He steadied himself, sent it on its way and, knees bent in anticipation, suddenly straightened in anguish as he saw the ball drift a fraction right, and past the hole. Cue wild American celebrations.

Most people had never heard of the 'yips' before this – but Langer's agonising miss at the 18th hole at Kiawah Island increased everyone's vocabulary and handed the Ryder Cup back to the USA.

Las Vegas Comes to Wimbledon

IT WAS just so right that Andre Agassi won his first Grand Slam title at Wimbledon. It was snooty, old-fashioned, English establishment meets brash, long-haired American (little did we know at the time that it was a wig). You could just see the members squirming in their seats. But the Centre Court crowd took Agassi to their hearts, as they often do an outsider.

Agassi had just plain refused to play Wimbledon for three years, in protest at the club's draconian dress code. So in 1992, resplendent in all white (albeit baggy shorts, shirt hanging loose and ponytail poking through his cap), he showed them what he was all about. And it was brilliant to watch him win it from the baseline, in the midst of an era of big servers. He beat two former champions, Boris Becker and John McEnroe, to get to the final. There, despite Goran Ivanisevic pounding down no fewer than 37 aces, Agassi's brilliant returning ability, strength and eye for a shot prevailed over five exhausting sets. Then he got to dance with Steffi Graf, his future wife.

Sadly, it was the only time we saw his genius, his guts, winning a Wimbledon final. Pistol Pete Sampras soon took over Centre Court, beating the Las Vegan in 1999. Pat Rafter accounted for him in two unforgettable semi-finals. In 2006 Agassi bowed out at the hands of Rafael Nadal, the emblem of a new generation. But boy, did he entertain us.

With his funny little legs and rock star haircut, no one knew what to make of Andre Agassi at first. But his tennis was sublime: he beat Becker and McEnroe on the way to victory in a thrilling five-set final with Goran Ivanisevic.

Mansell Leads from Start to Finish

IT WAS one of the most one-sided seasons ever but no one really minded. Nigel Mansell's utter domination of the rest of the field in 1992 gave Britain its first Formula One world drivers' title since 1976. To cap it all, although the championship was officially decided in Hungary in August, it was at Silverstone in July that the people came to crown their champion.

Mansell, back at Williams after a brief sojourn at Ferrari (but now no longer competing with Ayrton Senna), had won the first five races of the campaign. Senna and Gerhard Berger had picked up a couple of victories, but Mansell was back in his pomp again when the British Grand Prix arrived. He got pole, as usual – only Senna and the other Williams driver, Riccardo Patrese,

beat Mansell in qualifying all year. He led from start to finish, and at that finish, the crowd swarmed on to the track.

The fans' joy was unconfined, as befits a home Grand Prix winner. Martin Brundle making it on to the podium as well made it an even better day for Britain. Even Damon Hill got in on the act – he made his first Formula One start that day. And Mansell's victory was definitive in another way. He surpassed Jackie Stewart's tally of race wins to become Britain's most successful driver.

You might not be familiar with the Williams-Renault FW14B, but in the hands of a driver of the calibre of Nigel Mansell it was the fastest car in Formula One by miles in 1992.

The Golden Games

Linford was just so driven, so focused, in his prime ...

IF YOU can forgive the Freddie Mercury song, which grated ever so slightly after a fortnight, Barcelona was a great Olympics. The atmosphere seemed genuinely festive, a celebration of sport without quite so many commercial trappings.

Of all the Olympic medals to win, gold in the 100 metres is the ultimate, and for the first time since Allan Wells in Moscow in 1980, this time with the Americans there too, we had our world-beater. Linford Christie – lunchbox and all.

Linford was just so driven, so focused, in his prime: in beating the likes of Frankie Fredericks and Leroy Burrell, in going under the magic 10 seconds. We tend to forget that he was 32, definitely on the old side in his event, but his career was only really just getting going. Whatever doubts surround his performances, the fact is that Christie won more medals than any other male British athlete and fully deserves his place as Britain's greatest ever sprinter.

Ready. Set. BANG … Linford Christie ran the 100 metres in 9.96 seconds, winning gold and, at 32, becoming the oldest winner of the Olympic 100 metres by four years.

A few days later the British women's team captain Sally Gunnell crouches on the blocks waiting to start the race of her life. Her rival for 400 metres hurdles gold, American Sandra Farmer-Patrick, is one lane to her right. Bang! Then again. False start. She crouches once more. Bang! They're off. Gunnell is first to rise to hurdle No. 1 but by halfway, Farmer-Patrick is leading. Keeping her concentration, Gunnell alternates her leading leg over the last four hurdles. With three to go, she is level with the American and is the first, just, over the penultimate obstacle. She takes the last cleanly, 2 metres in front, and powers over the finish line where her mile-wide golden smile endears her even more to the public back home.

Sometimes it really is the taking part, not the winning, that counts. Who won the 400 metres in

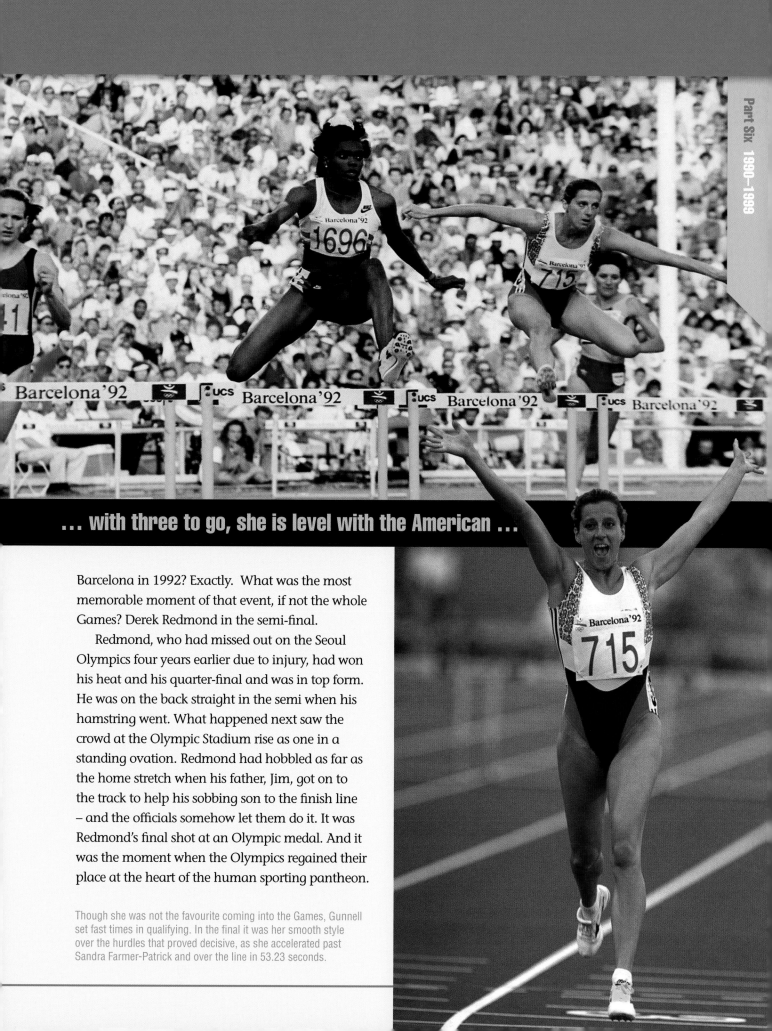

... with three to go, she is level with the American ...

Barcelona in 1992? Exactly. What was the most memorable moment of that event, if not the whole Games? Derek Redmond in the semi-final.

Redmond, who had missed out on the Seoul Olympics four years earlier due to injury, had won his heat and his quarter-final and was in top form. He was on the back straight in the semi when his hamstring went. What happened next saw the crowd at the Olympic Stadium rise as one in a standing ovation. Redmond had hobbled as far as the home stretch when his father, Jim, got on to the track to help his sobbing son to the finish line – and the officials somehow let them do it. It was Redmond's final shot at an Olympic medal. And it was the moment when the Olympics regained their place at the heart of the human sporting pantheon.

Though she was not the favourite coming into the Games, Gunnell set fast times in qualifying. In the final it was her smooth style over the hurdles that proved decisive, as she accelerated past Sandra Farmer-Patrick and over the line in 53.23 seconds.

Ball of the Century

NEVER HAS a man announced his arrival on the sporting scene in such a dramatic fashion. The First Test of the 1993 Ashes series, at Old Trafford. England had done well to get Australia out for 289 and were going on nicely at 80-1, despite having just lost the wicket of Michael Atherton, caught behind off the bowling of Merv Hughes. Now Allan Border decided it was time for some spin.

Shane Warne. He was meant to be a bit tasty. Up he shuffled, and his first ball veered from outside leg to hit Mike Gatting's off stump. Even umpire Dickie Bird could not believe it. You had to watch the replay to fathom what had happened. Surely no one could spin a ball like that? Oh yes, he could.

Warne would go on to claim the wickets of Robin Smith and England captain Graham Gooch to swing the match – and the series – Australia's way, but that was not even the half of it. He single-handedly tormented the opposition. He revived the art of leg-spin. He made cricket a game worth watching again. All the way up to the 2005 Ashes, when England finally got their hands back on the urn, the sport became something much more than just a contest. For more than one reason, thank goodness Shane Warne's in the commentary box now.

Mike Gatting's red face and puzzled expression says it all, as Shane Warne's first ball in Test cricket rips across the pitch and clatters into his stumps. It was the first of many.

146

Offiah Even Impresses Himself

FOR A start, he had the best nickname in sport – 'Chariots' Offiah. It was bestowed because of his unbelievable speed and strength through the tackle. Leeds were well aware of his qualities ahead of their 1994 Challenge Cup final showdown with Wigan. Offiah's ten tries against them in 1992 had set a new benchmark for annihilation (although Shaun Edwards, not a man to be outdone, soon reached double figures himself against Swinton). Playing Wigan prior to Offiah's arrival in 1992 had been bad enough – now all you could do was try and stop him getting the ball. Tricky, especially when he received it at the play-the-ball.

Of all Offiah's tries, running the length of the field at Wembley in 1994 summed the man up. A quick burst, then past flailing Leeds' arms, and the legs really stretched.

A look around, then another astonishing burst, Alan Tait left in his wake. It was only 12 minutes in, but the game was already over – and even after all Offiah's tries, you could see what it meant to him, and how good he knew it had been to watch.

Wigan won their seventh straight Challenge Cup. A month later, the Brisbane Broncos were defeated on home soil in the World Club Challenge. Wigan was the supreme team of a generation; Offiah the destroyer. That performance even earned him another decent nickname – the Aussies called him 'Great Balls'.

Martin Offiah – the man with the best nicknames in sport – clutches his head in wonder after scoring a brilliant opening try against Leeds in 1994.

Death of a Legend

DEATH IN sport is something we have all had to come to terms with. Losing your life in the pursuit of what is effectively entertainment renders the nature of healthy competition irrelevant. And yet a dark seam of tragedy lies within the golden moments sport produces, and there have been few worse weekends than at San Marino in 1994.

It was the third Grand Prix of the season. Michael Schumacher had won the first two races; Ayrton Senna was in pole position for the third time, but by Sunday, the event was already shrouded in sorrow. In practice on the Friday, Senna's fellow Brazilian Rubens Barrichello had suffered a horrific crash but, miraculously, suffered no lasting damage. The next day, the Austrian driver Roland Ratzenberger was not so lucky. His car failed to turn at the Villeneuve corner and hit a concrete wall at 195mph. No chance. But his death would be overshadowed on race day by that of Senna, the three-times world champion.

After two laps at racing speed – the first five laps had been under the safety car following an accident on the starting line – Senna's Williams, the leading car at the time, failed to turn at Tamburello corner, running in a straight line off the track and into an unprotected concrete barrier at 190mph. He died shortly after impact from a severe head injury. Half a million people lined the streets of São Paulo for his funeral. The main memory of the man will always be his genius, not the debris at Imola. And at least his legacy – as the last driver to die in a Formula One race – will be the safety measures that came too late to save him.

Monumental genius, frightening commitment, and a willingness to go right to the very edge forged Ayrton Senna da Silva into one of Formula One's greatest drivers.

Jimmy White Gets a New Nickname

JIMMY WHITE must rue the day that Stephen Hendry first picked up a snooker cue. The pair met on four occasions in the World Championship final, and Hendry won each time. The first, in 1990, saw the Scot become the youngest player ever to win the title. In the second, two years later, White took a 14-8 lead, then proceeded to lose the next ten frames and the match. In 1993, Hendry swept White away and won with a session to spare. Then came their final encounter for the greatest prize in the game.

The match went to the very last frame, after White had produced a dazzling 75 break to come back from 17-16 down. With the momentum now with the Whirlwind, and the majority of fans in the arena and watching on television willing him to win, he produced some phenomenal snooker in the most tense of situations to take a 37-24 lead, with the balls well placed. Surely this time the world crown was his, his destiny. But destiny had other plans for Jimmy White.

It seems the fickle fates wanted to bestow another nickname on the man from Tooting. Lining up a regulation (even given the circumstances) black into the bottom right corner, White jabbed at it and missed. Hendry produced a master class to clear the table and record his fourth world crown. Destiny's nickname? Jimmy 'The greatest player never to win the world title' White.

Jimmy White buries his face in a towel as Stephen Hendry clears the table, wins the frame and the world title … for the fourth time in their four encounters.

'You Guys are History'

FOR MOST of its history, English cricket has lacked a really fast bowler. The kind who terrifies, intimidates, and preferably skittles out the opposition. But at the Oval in 1994, we finally saw it: wild fury, vicious vengeance.

South Africa were the opposition, and after the first innings, England captain Mike Atherton had berated Devon Malcolm for his display – an inconsistent 1 for 81. Malcolm was the rabbit in the England batting order, but for some reason, Fanie de Villiers decided he was worth a bouncer. It struck the Jamaica-born, Derbyshire quickie on the helmet. He was not happy. 'You guys are history,' he announced to the watching South African slip cordon, and was soon steaming in to wreak havoc.

Devon Malcolm celebrates after bowling Hansie Cronje and reducing South Africa to 1 for 3. He ended the innings with the incredible figures of 9 for 57. You don't mess with Devon.

In the most astonishing opening to a Test innings, Gary Kirsten was caught and bowled, his half-brother Peter mistimed a hook to Phil DeFreitas, and then Hansie Cronje's stumps were levelled before he had time to form a stroke. South Africa were 1 for 3! The wickets continued to tumble, the Oval crowd roared, and when Allan Donald was clean bowled, Malcolm's final analysis was 9 for 57. It was breathtaking, and no English fast bowler has ever come close to matching his performance.

Foggy Wins Down Under

CHARISMATIC, COMMITTED, controversial, versatile, determined, gutsy, a folk-hero – all words used to describe Carl Fogarty. But added to them must be 'super-charged talent'. In 1994 he proved that beyond doubt, in a season that should really have been about Foggy retaining his title. The previous year he had won 11 of the 26 races. Unfortunately he also crashed his Ducati many times and was beaten to the pennant by his arch-rival, American Scott Russell, who won only five races but crucially picked up points when Fogarty didn't. The following year, Foggy was determined to make amends. Not that you would have known it by the second round at Hockenheim. Fogarty was on the tarmac once again, suffering a broken wrist that meant three weeks later he was racing with a cast. By round four he was 56 points behind Russell, but four wins on the trot clearly marked his intentions. Going into the final two races, in Australia, Foggy had a five-point lead. A win in the first extended this to eight and when the American retired with a technical problem in the final race, the first of Foggy's four World Superbike Championships was his, on the track that five years later was to end his career. Chasing a third consecutive title in April 2000 Foggy suffered a near-death crash that left him with multiple fractures and muscles that could no longer perform to the level a world champion requires.

Foggy takes the plaudits as he wins the final race and the 1994 World Superbike Championship. He retired in 2000 with a career record of 59 race victories and four world championships.

'A Most Unsporting Moment'

In an extraordinary manoeuvre Schumacher (right) and Hill crash out of the Australian Grand Prix, ensuring a championship victory for the German driver. Deliberate or not, the incident was included in a 2003 BBC poll of the 'most unsporting moments'.

THE 1994 Formula One season proved to be one of the most controversial in the history of the sport. And one of the most tragic. Michael Schumacher's Benetton won six of the first seven races, giving him a seemingly unassailable lead over Damon Hill in the Williams. But the dreadful loss of Roland Ratzenberger and Ayrton Senna at San Marino cast a long shadow over the championship and seemed to foretell dark days ahead for the German driver and his team.

First Schumacher ignored a black flag at Silverstone, for failing to come in for a stop-and-go penalty. He lost the race points and received a two-race suspension. Then his team were caught twice for technical illegalities – on their launch control and fuelling systems – followed by a further disqualification, in Belgium, as a result of the non-regulation floor of his car.

The championship came down to the final race in Australia, with Hill a point behind his rival. In the wet–dry conditions, with Schumacher defending his lead and Hill climbing all over his back, they battled for 36 laps, until the German drifted wide and touched a wall. Hill moved to overtake and Schumacher tried to block. In so doing he smashed into the Williams with such force that the Benetton pivoted on to two tyres and both men were out. Deliberate? Unsporting? Who can say? An indication of his ruthless will to win? Almost certainly. Schumacher was champion, and he rightly dedicated his victory to Senna.

Milton the Wonder Horse

WITH HIS trademark leap into the air, the world's first £1 million show jumper bade goodbye to his countless fans and to competitive life at the Olympia Show Jumping Championships in December 1994. Milton, the wonderful grey, had won almost everything there was to win in the sport and deserved his ovation, having given such pleasure to so many.

Bred for show jumping and synonymous with John Whitaker, Milton was originally bought by Caroline Bradley who was convinced she had found her Olympic horse. Tragically, she never had the chance to find out, dying suddenly at the age of 37, when Milton was only six years old. With Whitaker on his back from 1985, Milton honoured his original owner's ability and knowledge by jumping without equal, entertaining royally and winning magnificently, including Nations Cups,

Grands Prix, individual and team gold in the 1989 European Championships and the World Cup finals of 1990 and 1991.

The only major prizes to evade Milton were the Olympics, when in Barcelona in 1992 he had a shot at individual gold but failed at the double oxer, and the World Championship, although he did win individual silver in the 1990 competition in Stockholm. But such gaps in his trophy cabinet did not matter one bit. Milton was beloved and rightly so. He spent his retirement with his friend Hopscotch and died in 1999. As Whitaker said of him, he was 'Simply the Best'.

Milton, voted 'Britain's best loved horse' in 2008, had true star quality and, in the capable hands of John Whitaker, became show jumping's first millionaire.

Cantona Sees Red

WAS EVERYONE kung fu fighting? Well, Eric Cantona was. He had been sent off following a petulant kick at Crystal Palace defender Richard Shaw and was being escorted along the touchline when he reacted to comments made by Matthew Simmons, a Palace supporter who had come down from his seat 11 rows back to heckle the Frenchman. Cantona broke free of his minders and leapt across the advertising hoardings to slam his right foot into his tormentor's chest (the act famously described as a 'kung fu kick') before scrambling back to his feet to follow up with a right hook. The football world was shocked. Regardless of the level of provocation, and no one denied the abuse spewed out at Cantona was extremely unpleasant, there was no excuse for such a reaction. Simmons was sentenced to

seven days' imprisonment for abusive language and behaviour (he served one day). For his part, Cantona was stripped of the French captaincy, banned from football for nine months (United initially banned him for the rest of that season – a championship they lost to Blackburn on the final day) and, having been first sentenced to a jail term, eventually undertook community service. When facing the press following his conviction, Cantona had only one statement to make. 'When the seagulls follow the trawler it's because they think sardines will be thrown into the sea.' That clears things up then, Eric.

Tempers were running high when Eric Cantona (in black) attacked abusive Palace fan Matthew Simmons after being sent off. It was an incident that both player and supporter have come to regret.

Nayim from the Halfway Line

OF ALL the unwritten laws of football, that which states that a returning player shall score against his former club is actually set in stone. A twist in this law takes on an added dimension when a player who used to play for your greatest rivals returns to score against you. Arsenal will for ever be tormented by 'Nayim from the halfway line'.

The Gunners were aiming to be the only club ever to retain the European Cup-Winners' Cup, a trophy Alan Smith's goal had secured against Parma in Copenhagen 12 months previously. But this was an Arsenal team in transition. George Graham was gone, bunged out of the club. Wenger was still 'Arsène Who?' Caretaker manager Stewart Houston had supplemented the Gunners' famous back four with Andy Linighan. But they should still beat this Real Zaragoza team, surely.

(Left) In his book *Safe Hands*, David Seaman recalled, '… as soon as he struck it I knew I was in trouble'; (right) and despite his efforts the ball looped over the Arsenal keeper and into the net for the winner.

Back then, of course, Spanish football was hardly ever on our screens and their players were unknown. So it was perhaps inevitable, after John Hartson's equaliser in the Parc des Princes and a full 30 minutes of extra time, that Nayim – five and a half years at Spurs, including being Paul Gascoigne's replacement in the 1991 FA Cup final – should decide it. Nayim from the halfway line, Seaman back-pedalling but too late to stop the ball looping into the top of the net. It was an uncanny precursor for David Seaman and England against Brazil in 2002. And yes, the chant does scan perfectly.

Jonah Lomu Brushes England Aside

THIS WAS only Jonah Lomu's sixth cap for the All Blacks and, although he had shown more than just flashes of his ability in New Zealand's wins over the other three home nations in the previous rounds of the World Cup, England were confident they could contain him. Their last-gasp victory, thanks to a Rob Andrew drop-goal, over reigning champions Australia in the quarter-final had understandably given them a considerable boost. It was perhaps over-demonstrated by Tony Underwood's wink to Lomu at the end of the haka.

Within two minutes Lomu's power and speed were on full display. Picking up a pass on the left wing, he brushed off Underwood, sped past captain Will Carling and charged straight through a despairing Mike Catt for the first of his four tries. Twenty-five minutes into the game and the contest was over. A further Lomu try, in addition to a score from Josh Kronfeld and an audacious drop-goal from Zinzan Brooke, put the All Blacks out of sight. England rallied to inject some degree of respectability into the score, 45-29, but the All Blacks were heading for their famous encounter with hosts South Africa in Johannesburg.

To his credit, Underwood (and his mother and brother) took the demolition well, later appearing with Lomu in a TV ad for pizza, in which at least one Underwood eventually managed to floor the big man with a tackle – Mrs Underwood.

Described by the English press as 'a rhinoceros in ballet shoes', Lomu makes short work of his marker Tony Underwood to score the first of his four semi-final tries.

Mandela Wins it for South Africa

In one of sport's most emotional moments, Nelson Mandela prepares to hand the Rugby World Cup to the winning captain.
Mandela: 'François, thank you for what you have done for our country.'
Pienaar: 'No, Mr President. Thank you for what you have done.'

EVER SINCE Michael Caine took on the Zulus, Britain and South Africa have hardly been the best of friends. But the whole of the country – the whole of the planet, in fact – was united behind the men in green when they took on the All Blacks in the 1995 Rugby World Cup final.

The reason was simple: Nelson Mandela. It was five years since his release from life imprisonment. Two years since he won the Nobel Peace Prize. A year since he became president and apartheid was finally consigned to history. This World Cup was about far more than rugby. It was a showcase for the new South Africa, of course, but most of all it was a chance for the world to see the astonishing effect that one man had on a nation.

Mandela, arguably, could not have done this without François Pienaar. The inspirational Springboks captain had enormous respect for Mandela; he was his spokesman within the team and he transformed the most hardcore of Afrikaans arenas, Ellis Park, into a celebration of the Rainbow Nation. Pienaar was a brilliant player too, of course, and the negation of Jonah Lomu and New Zealand in the final was largely down to the captain and his back-row, plus scrum-half Joost van der Westhuizen.

Joel Stransky's extra-time drop-goal officially won the Webb Ellis Trophy. It was Mandela who won the hearts and minds though. There was not a dry eye in the house.

Edwards Soars into the Record Books

GREAT BRITAIN won just one gold medal in the 1995 World Athletics Championships, but Jonathan Edwards' performance in Gothenburg was of such a level that his world record in the triple jump still stands to this day.

By 1995, Edwards was already the absolute best at his event, untouchable. He had started the summer by setting a new UK record of 17.58 metres in Loughborough, then soared past 18 metres (with the aid of a strong tailwind, unfortunately) at the European Cup in June. Even then, he could not believe the distances he was doing. At a meeting in Salamanca in Spain, he captured the world record with a leap of 17.98. Edwards became a household name. Every record

attempt was live on television. But that sunny August evening in Sweden, he really nailed it.

With astonishing speed on the runway, yet a lightness of touch and a grace beyond compare, Edwards' first jump took him out to 18.16 metres. The stadium erupted. The gold medal was secured. But Edwards was not satisfied, he knew he was flying, and in his very next attempt he extended his record to 18.29. Sheer brilliance. It was beyond the markers, beyond what any man could jump. He remains the only British man to hold an athletics world record.

Jonathan Edwards flies through the Gothenburg air, landing at 18.29 metres. He set a new triple jump world record, one that still stands today.

Colin McRae Wins in Style

LANARK-BORN Colin McRae only knew two speeds: flat-out or out-flat. It was this 'win or crash' mentality, coupled with brilliant natural ability, which produced the flamboyant, exuberant, passionate and spectacular drives that made his name. If McRae didn't win, there was a fair chance he didn't finish. Fortunately, his skill outshone his sometimes crazy streak, allowing him to chalk up 25 rally wins in his career.

Driving for Subaru, McRae won his first World Rally Championships race in 1993 and by 1995, with his co-driver Derek Ringer, he was a leading contender for the title. His season started poorly, with retirements in the first two races; but a third place in Portugal, first in New Zealand, and second in both Australia and Spain saw him

Colin McRae hit the heights to win the RAC Rally in 1995, coming home 36 seconds ahead of his teammate and nearest rival Carlos Sainz in a race that many believe was his greatest ever.

storm back. By the final race – the RAC Rally in Wales in November – he was joint-leader with teammate Carlos Sainz. The winner-takes-all showdown suited McRae and in a close battle he prevailed over his rival by 36 seconds to become the youngest winner of the title and Britain's first.

Perhaps the most surprising aspect of McRae's blistering career was that 1995 was his only world title, though he came close in 1996 and 2001. Arguably, his devil-may-care style cost him those championships, but it won him an army of fans, fans who in 2007 were devastated to learn of their hero's death in a tragic helicopter accident.

Atherton's Captain's Innings

PATIENCE IS a virtue much treasured in a Test match cricketer, and England captain Mike Atherton had it in abundance on the winter tour to South Africa in 1995. The home team could hardly have been hungrier for the series – the end of apartheid brought England to South Africa for their first official tour since the sporting ban was imposed – and in Allan Donald and the debutant Shaun Pollock they had a fearsome pair of fast bowlers.

Rain wrote off the First Test, so it was in Johannesburg that battle really commenced. Skittled for 200 first time out, England were set 479 to win, in the best part of two days. Time for a rearguard action, a captain's innings. And what an innings it was. Atherton batted for 10 hours and 43 minutes, facing 492 balls for his 185 not out, but it was by no means just defence.

Hooking bouncers when he could (and getting hit in the process), Atherton smashed 15 boundaries for his century, the final one after being dropped on 99. The emotion spilled out as he embraced Robin Smith, but it was when he was joined at the wicket by Jack Russell that the pair found an astonishing zone. There was just no removing them. They were confident, they were supreme, they battled on to earn the draw and it made every English supporter feel very, very proud.

Determined, brave and single-minded, Mike Atherton was always up for a battle. Stubborn defensive play was his main weapon, but hooking and cutting through point helped him reach 185 not out to save the Second Test against South Africa in 1995.

Shaun Edwards – End of an Era

WHEN WIGAN wrapped up their seventh straight league title with a win against Bradford in January 1996, it was hard to foresee just how much the sport of rugby league was about to change. What could almost be sensed in the Central Park air that Tuesday night, though, was that it was the end of an era. An era of unprecedented domination by a team that had long since gone beyond superlatives.

Shaun Edwards, as ever, was at the heart of it all, feeding tries for the likes of Va'aiga Tuigamala, Henry Paul, Martin Offiah and Kris Radlinski. Gary Connolly and Jason Robinson completed what was a simply phenomenal set of backs (although Andy Gregory might have a word to say about that). Other Wigan greats

were no longer there – Denis Betts, Dean Bell – but Edwards, the heart and soul of Wigan, could take in the moment. Edwards and Wigan had smashed everything in their path, all the records and, famously, the captain's cheekbone in the 1990 Challenge Cup final.

Here, now, was the end of a hundred years of winter rugby, a curtailed season (the Stones Bitter Centenary Championship, no less!) before the advent of the Super League. Wigan would soon become the Warriors. But not in the way that this team were.

The real Wigan warrior – Shaun Edwards (second left) led British rugby league's most successful club during its most successful era.

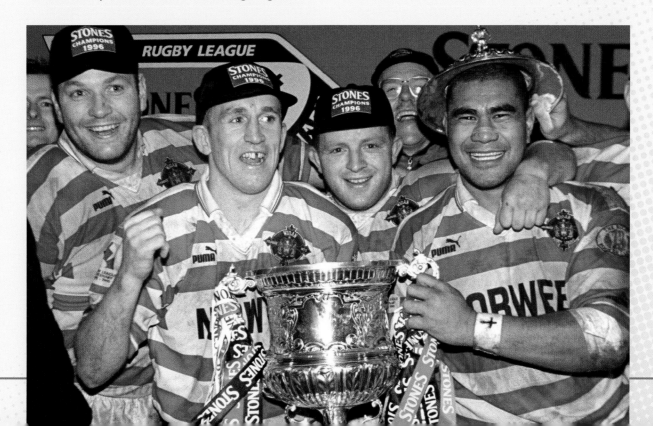

Faldo Reels in the White Shark

SIX SHOTS behind the world No. 1, Nick Faldo surely had no chance to claim his sixth Major at the 1996 Masters. A birdie on the last green of the third round had ensured that Faldo partnered leader Greg Norman. In Faldo's mind, the final round was match play, and given his magnificent Ryder Cup record in that format, well... In addition, Norman had led seven times going into the last round of a Major, and had only won once.

Norman's bogie on the first gifted Faldo the perfect start. From there it got steadily worse for the popular Australian. He took longer and longer over his shots, never settling into his grip, never settling at all. By the 11th, after Norman carded four bogeys in a row, they were all square. Then it got really bad. He found water at the 12th; Faldo went two in front. By now, the White Shark was cutting a forlorn figure and the galleries hardly knew where to look. Water again at the 16th sealed Norman's fate. Faldo sank his final putt to complete an inspired 67 and in a show of great respect he barely celebrated, choosing instead to hug the popular Australian. Words were exchanged, provoking tears from both. It is impossible to say what impact the events had on both men, but one thing is certain, neither won a Major again.

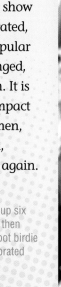

In the final round Faldo made up six strokes in 11 holes – Norman then double bogeyed twice. A 20-foot birdie putt at the last and Faldo celebrated the sixth Major of his career.

Keegan's Meltdown

YOU COULD almost imagine Alex Ferguson sitting at home having watched title rivals Newcastle defeat Leeds 1-0, savouring a fine red and quietly humming John Lennon's classic 'Mind Games'. The Magpies' win brought them within three points of the leaders Manchester United and with a game in hand, but you suspect Fergie wouldn't have been overly worried about that. His focus will have been on Newcastle manager Kevin Keegan's post-match interview with Andy Gray and Richard Keys back in the Sky studio.

Over the previous weeks, as the title race tightened, the United boss employed his full repertoire of psychological tricks, suggesting that in the final run-in certain teams would not try as hard as they might against Newcastle. On the back of a three-match winning streak, this proved too much for Keegan, whose pent-up emotion was clear for all to see. It was perhaps mixed with a hint of frustration at having let a 12-point lead at Christmas slip.

With finger jabbing at the screen and words tumbling out in a jumble, Keegan handily pointed out to Ferguson that United still had to get something out of their final match of the season against Middlesbrough, before telling the world, honestly, that he would love it, love it if Newcastle beat them.

They didn't and as Ferguson lifted the trophy you could imagine he still had the words of John Lennon's song playing on his lips.

A man under pressure: Kevin Keegan (second left) tries to make sense of it all as Newcastle's title challenge peters out and United overhaul them in the last few matches of the 1995-96 season.

Football Comes Home (Well, Almost)

LET'S FACE it, the last great international football tournament was Euro '96. One of the special things about it was that England really was 100 per cent behind the team, despite the lame draw with Switzerland in the opening match. The whole country was resplendent with St George's flags when Scotland came to Wembley for the next match on a glorious summer's day.

On that day came that goal and that dentist's chair celebration. Teddy Sheringham's deft pass to a breaking Paul Gascoigne (just after David Seaman had saved Gary McAllister's penalty), the flick over Colin Hendry's head and then the volley rocketing past Andy Goram in the Scotland goal: 2-0, game over.

Manager Terry Venables had put together quite a team: combative (Pearce, Adams, Ince), proven goalscorers (Shearer, Sheringham), together with one of England's more creative midfields

Euro '96 – the last great international football tournament, at least from an English point of view, saw the country awash with St George's flags.

(Anderton, McManaman). And then Gazza, the maverick genius who may have got lashed on a night out in Hong Kong but back then that was no obstacle to his performance on the field.

Another trademark celebration, copied by kids up and down the country, came in the next match. One arm in the air, peeling away from the goalmouth, soon followed by the roar of 'Shear-er' round the stadium. With Alan Shearer and Teddy Sheringham up front, England had one of their best strike forces, and one of their finest games ever, against the Netherlands.

It all came down to a 12-minute spell early in the second half. After Sheringham had headed past Edwin van der Sar for England's second came the goal that really capped the display. Paul

Gascoigne skipping into the box, dinking it with his right foot to Sheringham, in plenty of space by the penalty spot. A nonchalant right-footed pass to Shearer, in yet more space, and the No. 9 lashed the ball into the net. The 4-1 win is still England's finest Wembley performance since a certain game in 1966. It's no wonder we are so nostalgic about it.

That day came that goal and that dentist's chair celebration.

The quarter-final against Spain had another moment of high drama, after 120 minutes with no goals and little else to commend it. England were lucky to still be in it as the Spaniards had a goal disallowed for no apparent reason. Penalties. Spain hit the bar and then Stuart Pearce walked to the spot to show the world what he was made of. In Italia '90 he had taken the same lonely path after England and Germany had battled to a 1-1 draw after extra-time. With the scores 3-3 and a place in the final at stake, Pearce had sent his spot-kick down the middle, to be met by the trailing legs of Bodo Illgner. Taxi for England.

The devastation felt by this fiercely proud Englishman that night in Turin was clear for all to see, and when he stepped up once again, at Wembley, the nation held its breath. They needn't have worried. With no trace of nerves, he smashed his penalty into the bottom left-hand corner of the net, then turned to the crowd, pumping his fists and roaring in a primeval surge of relief and redemption. 'Psycho' had stepped from behind the shower curtain to be counted and he didn't let anyone down. Pure guts.

Of course, it all went wrong after that: in the semis we lost to Germany, on penalties.

England had a number of stars in action at Euro '96, not least Gazza and his goal against Scotland (top), and Stuart Pearce (right) whose penalty against Spain provided passion when we needed it most.

Beckham Comes of Age

IF IT was not exactly the moment when David Beckham became a household name – he had, after all, won the League and Cup Double the previous season. It was when he announced himself. In typical fashion: flamboyant, self-assured. Unusually for what was to come in his career though, it happened on a small stage, in south London.

Manchester United had three points in the bag against Wimbledon, 2-0 up through first-half goals from Eric Cantona and Denis Irwin. It was the 90th minute of a routine opening day victory. But the third goal, and the face of United's No. 10 (Cantona had the divine right to No. 7) would soon be beamed across the globe. It was a glorious goal, the 21-year-old Beckham spotting Neil Sullivan off his line and flighting the ball perfectly over the Dons' keeper from the halfway line. A shoe-in for Premier League Goal of the Decade, but it became even more than that.

Five days later, Beckham was named in Glenn Hoddle's first England squad, making his debut against Moldova. United won the Premier League, Beckham was named Young Player of the Year, Cantona left and Beckham inherited the No. 7 shirt. He met and later married a pop star. A global superstar was born.

The shape of things to come: David Beckham, 21 years old, supremely confident in his ability, takes the plaudits after his spectacular goal against Crystal Palace.

Frankie's Magnificent Seven

ON 28 September 1996, seven was a lucky number not just for Frankie Dettori, but for the thousands of punters who backed the popular Italian jockey to ride winners. His achievement of going through the seven-race card at Ascot stripped the bookmakers of something in the region of £50 million.

On the morning of the meeting, Dettori said that he thought he could have an each-way chance in the first race, and was confident of a win in the third, the Queen Elizabeth Stakes. After riding Wall Street and Diffident, by the shortest of heads, to victory, a late burst by Mark of Esteem made it three in a row. Decorated Hero, a 7-1 shot, made it four, and was followed by wins on Fatefully and Lochangel. Only the Gordon Carter Handicap remained. Fujiyama Crest was Dettori's mount, top weight in the race, but lifted by a roar from the grandstand he kept going and going to win by a neck. The odds on Dettori winning the straight set were 25,095-1. The odds are that no one will ever do it again.

The height of Frankie Dettori's trademark flying dismount apparently depends on how he feels about the victory he's celebrating – imagine how high he jumped after the seventh win in seven races at Ascot in September 1996.

Ronnie O'Sullivan – Fastest 147 Break

THE WORD 'genius' is bandied about too loosely, but when Ronnie O'Sullivan appeared on the snooker scene, we knew that we were in the presence of someone who would go on to redefine the sport. The Rocket had broken records from an early age – his first century at the age of ten, a maximum at 15. Two years later, O'Sullivan won the UK Championship, beating Stephen Hendry in the final.

By 21, he was already starting to experiment in major tournaments to keep his interest going, a trait that would make him wonderful to watch, if dangerously unpredictable. And at the World Championships at the Crucible in 1997, in the first round, against Mick Price, we saw the Rocket

One of the most successful snooker players in history, Ronnie O'Sullivan holds the record for the fastest professional 147 break at an average rate of one shot every 8.8 seconds!

doing what he did best – a 147 break, in just five minutes and twenty seconds. At first he didn't even seem to be going that quickly, but as the reds disappeared the adrenaline kicked in, yet the positional play remained perfect.

The century came in four minutes. The final black made it tough to get on the yellow. Sorted. When the 147 was completed, the arena was full of pure joy. There were whistles, and odd celebrations – Ronnie even threw his chalk into the crowd – but most of all, he was just having a lot of fun.

Blink and You Missed It

CHELSEA HAD not won a major domestic honour since 1970. They had made it to the 1994 final, holding Manchester United for an hour, before crashing to a 4-0 defeat. Chelsea, vintage 1997, was a very different proposition. Ruud Gullit was manager, Gianfranco Zola had joined six months previously and they were beginning to combine flair with results, finishing sixth in the Premier League. Opposing them were a stubborn Middlesbrough side determined to salvage something from a relegation season. The start was going to be all important. Thirty-three seconds in, Dennis Wise robbed Juninho of the ball midway in Chelsea's half. He rolled a pass to Di Matteo who ran, and ran and ran. The Middlesbrough

All that build-up, all the hype, all the tension – relief and joy are writ large on the faces of Roberto di Matteo (left) and his Chelsea teammates as they take a 43-second lead against Middlesbrough.

defence backed off, falling hook, line and sinker for a clever decoy run by Mark Hughes. Thirty yards out, Di Matteo smashed a dipping shot, Ben Roberts flapped and missed, and in 43 seconds Chelsea were one up and on their way to victory thanks to the fastest goal in FA Cup history. Until …

In the 2009 final, Louis Saha scored in 25 seconds for Everton against Chelsea. But Di Matteo still holds the record for the fastest goal in an FA Cup final at the original Wembley, and three years later he also scored the last goal at the old stadium, for Chelsea against Aston Villa.

BOXING WBA World Heavyweight Championship
Mike Tyson v. Evander Holyfield, MGM Grand Garden Arena, Las Vegas, 28 June 1997

1997

Tyson Loses Control

Fight referee Mills Lane takes his life into his hands as he tells Tyson that the fight is over as a result of him biting a chunk out of Evander Holyfield's right ear.

IT WAS one of the most infamous moments in boxing, and the sport of kings has had its fair share. There was nothing fair, though, about Tyson–Holyfield in 1997. It was billed as 'The Sound and the Fury', but the only sound after the fight was the fury of the world directed at Iron Mike. And his bite.

By then, Tyson had been in and out of jail and had lost two bouts – to Buster Douglas in a stunning upset in 1990, and in another shock defeat to Evander Holyfield the previous year. Holyfield had been perceived as washed-up, too old, but he outboxed (and out-headbutted, it appeared) his rival. The WBA World Heavyweight Championship was again on the line. As with all rematches, the hype surrounding it was huge.

Tyson really came out fighting in the third round but it was clear he was wild, out of control. With the two men in a clinch, he took a chunk out of Holyfield's ear. From the microphones in the ring, you knew what had happened. The replays showed it. Unbelievable. Referee Mills Lane was stunned too, but let the fight continue, albeit briefly. This time, Tyson went for the other ear. And then paid the consequences.

Disqualification. Derision. The loss of his licence. The loss of any remaining dignity. Lennox Lewis would polish off Tyson's career, but this was the point of no return.

Guscott Makes Lions Roar

LIONS SERIES victories are rare and hard earned. There have only been two in the past eight tours. But no one reading the press before the 1997 Lions headed off to South Africa would have imagined they would come back with one of them.

This was the first Lions tour of the professional era, and if the world seemed to be writing them off, coach Ian McGeechan, manager Fran Cotton and the string of specialists they took with them were certainly not. Six ex-rugby league players were included in the squad, to add edge, and the thoroughness of the preparation was evident in the First Test in Cape Town. The Lions took the game to the Springboks and dominated, winning 25-16.

South Africa learned their lesson and the surprise factor had gone by the Second Test, which boiled down to defensive heroics and the ability/inability to kick for points. South Africa won 3-0 in tries, but missed every kick, while Neil Jenkins imperiously slotted home five penalties to keep the match level at 15-15 with four minutes to go.

The Lions won a line-out inside the Boks' 22, pushed on to within 5 metres of the line, and released Gregor Townsend. The Scot was held up short, but then Matt Dawson flighted the ball to Jeremy Guscott, who was positioned at stand-off and ready to drop-kick himself into Lions history. Cue one of the biggest smiles in world sport.

Guscott celebrates as his cool dropped goal brings an 18-15 Test victory over South Africa in Durban to wrap up the series for the British & Irish Lions.

The Match That Had Everything

TWELVE YEARS after the 'Hand of God', England were looking for revenge against Argentina in the second round of the 1998 World Cup. Played in a fever-pitch atmosphere, the match was set alight immediately with David Seaman bringing down Diego Simeone for a sixth-minute penalty, which Gabriel Batistuta converted. Four minutes later, Owen tumbled in the box after the faintest (to be generous) of touches. Alan Shearer equalised.

Five minutes later, David Beckham fed Owen the ball as he stood in the centre circle, in the shadow of José Chamot. The teenager flicked it past him with the outside of his right boot, and set off towards goal at blistering pace, cutting into the box, knocking it past a bewildered Roberto Ayala and then smashing the ball past the helpless Carlos Roa. But Argentina equalised with a clever free-kick just before the half-time break.

Two minutes into the second half, Simeone clattered into Beckham, leaving him lying face down right in front of the referee. The lad from Leytonstone flicked out his right foot and made contact with Simeone's calf. He staggered backwards and collapsed as if struck by a baseball bat. The blue-shirted Argentinians, in particular Batistuta, surrounded the ref, beseeching him to take action, a tactic employed earlier by the South Americans for their penalty. Simeone saw yellow. It was red for Beckham, greeted with an approving and (self-) satisfied nod from Batistuta.

England played the rest of the half and 30 minutes of extra time like men possessed, every one a hero. Then penalties. England scored three, but Ince and Batty missed; the Argentinians scored four. What a match! What a night! High drama, pure theatre. Owen came home a hero, Beckham to burning effigies.

It's one of those 'I was there' moments as Michael Owen ends a dazzling run with a dazzling goal to put England ahead against Argentina at St-Etienne.

Last-Gasp Glass

Goalkeeper Jimmy Glass (in red) celebrates his moment in the sun as his goal in the last minute of injury time on the final day of the season keeps Carlisle in the Football League.

IF YOU'RE going to have your 15 minutes of fame, they may as well be good ones. And as Jimmy Glass will tell you, the goal that he scored for Carlisle United on the final day of the 1998-99 season will never be anything short of legendary.

Carlisle needed a win at home against Plymouth Argyle to stay in the Football League. At 1-1, in the final minute of injury time, the Conference beckoned and celebrations had already started in Scarborough, who thought they were safe. Carlisle won a corner, up came their goalkeeper, and after his right-foot volley went in, from a rebound, a scene of bedlam erupted. It was the ultimate last-gasp escape, and it was shown on televisions all over the world.

The remainder of the story really tells you something about football. Glass, a journeyman keeper on loan from Swindon and only playing his third match, left the club, could not gain a decent contract anywhere, and soon departed from the game after drifting into non-league football. Scarborough went bust. Carlisle eventually did go down, but have bounced back up brightly, again becoming the pride of Cumbria. Glass is now a taxi driver in Dorset. But what a goal!

The Unprecedented Treble

THE INVOLVEMENT of English clubs in the latter stages of the Champions League has been so pervasive over the past decade that it can be hard to recall the novelty of Manchester United's appearance in the final against Bayern Munich in 1999 – the first for a Premiership side since the European ban following the Heysel Stadium disaster ten years before.

Alex Ferguson's unprecedented dream – he was still without the 'Sir' at the time – had begun on 14 April at Villa Park in the FA Cup semi-final replay against Arsenal, Ryan Giggs' wonder goal in extra time sealing their place in the final. On 16 May at Old Trafford United had to come from behind to beat Spurs 2-1 and take the league

Manchester United ended the 20th century with a season that summed up a hundred years of achievement: the class of Beckham (above), the goals of Sheringham (opposite top) and Solskjaer (opposite bottom) and the grit and drive of Roy Keane (with FA Cup) all played their part as the club swept everything before them.

title, Andy Cole's deft lob deciding matters in front of an ecstatic crowd. Newcastle offered little resistance in the FA Cup final at Wembley on 22 May. So, Double done, but the feeling at Old Trafford was of expectation of what was to come rather than satisfaction at what they had already achieved.

On to Barcelona, and the uncharted waters of the Champions League final, but without the suspended Paul Scholes and Roy Keane. And soon, United

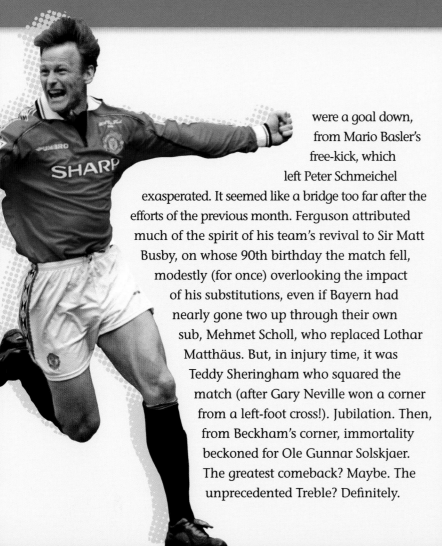

were a goal down, from Mario Basler's free-kick, which left Peter Schmeichel exasperated. It seemed like a bridge too far after the efforts of the previous month. Ferguson attributed much of the spirit of his team's revival to Sir Matt Busby, on whose 90th birthday the match fell, modestly (for once) overlooking the impact of his substitutions, even if Bayern had nearly gone two up through their own sub, Mehmet Scholl, who replaced Lothar Matthäus. But, in injury time, it was Teddy Sheringham who squared the match (after Gary Neville won a corner from a left-foot cross!). Jubilation. Then, from Beckham's corner, immortality beckoned for Ole Gunnar Solskjaer. The greatest comeback? Maybe. The unprecedented Treble? Definitely.

The greatest comeback? Maybe. The unprecedented Treble? Definitely.

Van de Velde Loses with Grace

IT'S EVERY golfer's dream. Standing on the 18th tee in the final round of the Open, requiring only a six to win. For Jean van de Velde, this dream turned into a nightmare.

First shot: the Frenchman smashes a risky drive into the semi-rough. Second: he dismisses a safe chip but his iron clatters the grandstand and disappears into thick grass. Third: Van de Velde's eyes are still set on the green but his attempt limps into the Barry Burn. Fourth: he discards shoes and socks, rolls up his trousers and goes for a paddle, but the ball sinks from view. Penalty drop. Fifth: he clears the burn, but not the bunker. Sixth: out of the sand and into the hole would do it. His playing partner, Craig Parry, is next to him in the bunker and incredibly does just that, but Van de Velde is unable to emulate him. Seventh: bravely, he makes an 8-foot putt for a play-off place. Events take their toll and Paul Lawrie, ten shots behind when he teed off, walks away as champion.

Foolhardy? Perhaps. But listening to Van de Velde reflect, it is impossible not to admire a man who went for his shots. 'What did you lose that day?' he was asked. 'I lost nothing. I play to win as a big dreamer, with what I can do myself. Not with something that is not me.' Winning with grace is pretty easy. Losing with it is a lot harder. He certainly did that.

Phlegmatic in defeat he might have been, but no one can forget the agony of watching Jean van de Velde get into every kind of trouble imaginable on a golf course at the 18th in Carnoustie.

Armstrong Beats Cancer to Win Tour

OPINIONS WILL always be divided about Lance Armstrong, but no one can deny the basic facts. Armstrong beat cancer, and won the Tour de France a record seven times.

The first of those victories, in 1999, was unbelievable. Armstrong had already served notice of his talent, winning his first Tour de France stage and the rainbow jersey of world champion at the age of 21, but his diagnosis with cancer in 1996 had surely put paid to that promising career. In fact, after all the treatment he underwent, Armstrong was lucky to be alive. But the Texan had a steely determination that went beyond normal parameters. The comeback began at the Vuelta a España in 1998: fourth

place. Then with his US Postal team in 1999, France was conquered. Armstrong's brilliance at time trialling set up the Tour victory, but, in a pattern that would soon become familiar, he won it in the mountains.

At the finish in Paris, Armstrong had his wife Kristin and mother Linda by his side. The next best rider, Alex Zülle, was more than seven and a half minutes adrift. It was the start of one of the most extraordinary achievements in sporting history.

Lance Armstrong rides past the Arc de Triomphe in Paris before riding up the Champs-Élysées in style to win his first Tour de France, three years after being diagnosed with testicular cancer.

Peter Nicol Wins Squash World Title

SQUASH IS all about timing and stamina. Knowing exactly when to flick the wrist, to retrieve dead balls from the back corner, and having the strength in your legs to reach them, time and time again. In 1999, Scotland's Peter Nicol showed both qualities.

Stamina: he was determined to lift the world title and refused to give up. Like Robert the Bruce's famous spider, Nicol tried (lost the 1997 final to Rodney Eyles), tried (lost the 1998 final to Jonathon Power) and tried again. Timing: why not wait to become world champion in the most spectacular setting imaginable, an open-air court in the shadow of the last remaining Wonder of the Ancient World, the Pyramids at Giza?

In his way stood the local hero and young pretender Ahmed Barada, roared on by the

A tough competitor, renowned for his excellent retrieving game, Peter Nicol is regarded as one of the most outstanding squash players of his time.

3,500-strong crowd, but no match for the Scot who won 15-9, 15-13, 15-11. Constantly on the defensive, Barada was given so few opportunities to score that he was unable to put together any sustained push. The one time he threatened to do so, leading 11-7 in the second game, Nicol merely switched up a gear and took the next seven points. British Open champion, Commonwealth gold medallist, World No. 1 and world champion, Scotland had a new sporting hero.

But not for long. Less than two years later, Nicol was swapping his Scottish thistle for the rose of England, citing lack of support from the Scottish authorities. How careless of them.

The Battle of Brookline

GOING INTO the final day of the 1999 Ryder Cup, Europe were sitting on a seemingly unassailable 10-6 lead. But there were glimmers of hope for the USA. Europe captain Mark James had chosen to employ all his big guns during the four previous rounds; fatigue would surely play a part. And in so doing, his three rookies – Andrew Coltart, Jarmo Sandelin and Jean van de Velde – had not yet been blooded; nerves would also surely play a part. So it transpired.

Europe lost the first six matches in devastating fashion, as the momentum swung unstoppably towards the Americans. It came down to the penultimate pairing, José María Olazábal against Justin Leonard, with the USA requiring only half a point to win the trophy. The Spaniard had been four up with seven to play, but on the 17th green, with Olazábal 20 feet from the pin, and Leonard a further 25 feet back, they were sitting all square.

Almost invisible in the long shadows, Leonard sent his putt scorching across the green. It appeared out of the shade, and disappeared into the hole. Leonard leapt with delight ... as did the caddies, players, and watching wives and girlfriends. Very soon they were on the green, dancing, hugging and cheering, while Olazábal waited to putt – to save the Ryder Cup. Needless to say, by the time the jamboree abated, the Spaniard's concentration was shot. He missed. The USA won with 14½ points. Both Europe and golf etiquette went home in tatters.

An astonishing comeback by the USA on the tournament's final day was ruined for many by the 'unsporting' behaviour of the winning team and the home galleries. This was typified by lengthy celebrations on the 17th green after Leonard's putt, with Olazábal still to putt to keep European hopes alive. Naturally he missed.

Part Seven
2000 | 2011

Super Caley ...

Thistle's Paul Sheerin steers his penalty past Celtic keeper Jonathan Gould and sends journalists away to come up with a seriously good headline for the Sunday paper.

'FREDDIE STARR ate my hamster', 'Zip me up before you go go' – both classic headlines in the *Sun*. But surely the best was reserved for the greatest upset in Scottish football. On 8 February 2000, part-timers Inverness Caledonian Thistle, with a history stretching back all of six years, travelled to Celtic Park for the third round of the Scottish Cup, to take on a club formed 112 years previously, littered with millionaire players, past European champions and one of the most famous teams in the world.

After 20 minutes, Caley were in front. A minute later Celtic equalised, but by half-time it was 2-1 to the Highlanders. What do the home faithful, who booed their team off the pitch, want to see in the second half? Fight, determination and certainly their top goalscorer. Sorry, 'fraid not. A half-time

dressing-room bust-up with manager John Barnes resulted in Mark Viduka failing to reappear. He was replaced by 36-year-old Ian Wright. The match was eventually wrapped up 3-1 through a Paul Sheerin penalty, leaving the visitors in dreamland and the home team with nightmares.

The following morning the world woke to copywriting genius: 'Super Caley go ballistic, Celtic are atrocious.' The result marked the end of Barnes's unhappy tenure at Celtic. It was a bitter pill to swallow for the ex-Liverpool legend in his first managerial role. One wonders if he took a spoonful of sugar when the Celtic board dished out his medicine.

Redgrave: The Great Olympian

'ANYONE SEES me go anywhere near a boat, you've got my permission to shoot me.' It was 1996 and Steve Redgrave and Matthew Pinsent had just won Olympic gold in the coxless pairs. For an exhausted Redgrave, that was it. But great competitors don't find it that easy to walk away. He started training again after four months off. He said it was agony, but that it proved he'd been right all through his career – true athletes can't have time off.

The run-up to the Sydney Games in 2000 was not without its problems. Redgrave was 38, suffering from colitis, and in 1997 had been diagnosed with diabetes. The effect on his training was catastrophic. A chipped elbow, a gashed hand, personal problems and a chronic back condition all featured. He had contemplated giving up his place in the boat.

Regardless, the four men made it to that Saturday morning for the final of the coxless fours. It took six minutes, 2,000 metres and around 240 strokes to make history. At 500 metres, the British team are under a second ahead of Australia; at 1,000 metres it is half a second. The time comes to push. Do they have it? Is Redgrave the weak link after all? With 250 metres to go, it is the Italians who are finishing strongest. Go again, go again, the British will themselves on. 'The Italians are coming!' screams the television commentary. They were. But not quite quickly enough. The result … an extraordinary and unprecedented fifth endurance gold for Redgrave, a third for Pinsent and the firsts for Tim Foster and James Cracknell.

Whatever you've got, we've got more: the British coxless four dig deep and hold on to win the gold medal in Sydney. Who looks the calmest? Redgrave (second from left), of course.

Paolo di Canio Plays Fair

Paolo di Canio accepts a special award from Everton's Paul Gerrard for his incredible gesture of stopping play rather than scoring with the goal at his mercy and the keeper on the ground injured.

COLOURFUL CHARACTER that he is, Paolo Di Canio was always going to provide us with some unforgettable moments. There was that volley against Wimbledon, an astounding piece of athleticism that deservedly won Goal of the Season; the infamous toppling of referee Paul Alcock when the Italian was at Sheffield Wednesday; some debatable goal celebrations at his beloved Lazio; but let's not pass by the gesture for which Di Canio won a FIFA Fair Play Award.

The Hammers looked to be taking a point from their trip to Everton when Toffees keeper Paul Gerrard went down in agony after clearing a ball. When Trevor Sinclair returned it to an unmarked Di Canio in the area, the goal was gaping. Goodison Park rose as one when the West Ham player caught the ball and pointed to Gerrard indicating that he needed treatment.

It was as surprising as it was a breath of fresh air in a Premier League tainted by gamesmanship – just the next month another goalkeeper, Fabien Barthez, would try to put Di Canio off scoring the only goal of West Ham's FA Cup win at Old Trafford. It was an early Christmas present for fans of football as it should be played. Di Canio is rightly loved by followers of football generally and not just West Ham fans for what he brings to the game: passion, pride and personality.

Ellen Against the Elements

SHE WAS the unlikeliest sporting icon, but Ellen MacArthur captured the nation's hearts in 2001 (even if she did lose out to David Beckham in the BBC Sports Personality of the Year award). Millions dropped what they were doing that Sunday evening in February just to watch the live coverage as her yacht *Kingfisher* crossed the finish line at Les Sables d'Olonne in France to complete the Vendée Globe, the toughest of all ocean races. She hadn't even won – a certain Michel Desjoyeaux took that honour, in a record time – but the exploits of the previous 94 days turned the soon-to-be Dame Ellen into a household name.

Solo, non-stop circumnavigation is always going to be an arduous experience, but MacArthur seemed to take it to extremes. The on-board cameras relayed every one of the 24-year-old's tears. It was just too much; she just couldn't take it any more. Every late-night repair, every mast-climb, was agony; the cold, the hunger, the loneliness. But on she persevered, even altering course to aid a stricken fellow sailor, and by the end of it all she was the youngest person, and first woman, to complete the race and sail so fast. More records would tumble in an extraordinary (and brief) sailing career for the redoubtable woman from land-locked Derbyshire. 'La Petite Anglaise' had conquered the world.

On-board cameras, radio reports, a newspaper diary and a logbook recorded Ellen's solo, non-stop circumnavigation of the globe in 2000-2001. Her arduous journey captured the hearts of the nation and she was welcomed home by huge crowds as she sailed up the Thames in London a few days later.

It's Owen's Day

DESPITE A pretty impressive record of 157 goals in 297 games for Liverpool, including a league-debut goal, Michael Owen is not too fondly remembered by the Anfield faithful. He was a star for England before Liverpool, moved on too soon and now wears a Manchester United shirt. What worse crimes could there be? But one day will live on in the hearts of all Reds – the 2001 FA Cup final against Arsenal.

Liverpool rode their luck on the day, as they had against Birmingham in winning the Worthington Cup back in February, with both Stéphane Henchoz (with his hand) and Sami Hyypia (more than once) clearing off the line even before Freddie Ljungberg gave Arsenal the lead. Sander Westerveld then denied Thierry Henry as the Gunners sought to seal it. But the tide turned when Robbie Fowler and Patrik

Curiously, for a superstar footballer, Michael Owen has never really hit the heights of popularity. But two goals in the last eight minutes for Liverpool against Arsenal in the 2001 FA Cup final ensured his place in the club's illustrious history.

Berger came on as substitutes and, with just eight minutes left, Owen lashed in an equaliser past David Seaman.

Jubilation reigned – just look at the goal celebration – and more was to come, in the moment when Owen did for Liverpool what he had for England in St-Etienne in 1998. Bursting down the field, he left defenders in his wake. A pinpoint finish. Pandemonium. Gérard Houllier's Liverpool would go on to win a Treble of cups. Just for once, it was Owen's day – how appropriate that it happened in the first FA Cup final to be played at the Millennium Stadium.

Liverpool Secure a Treble of their Own

IT WAS a cruel way to lose a European final – an own goal with just three minutes of extra time remaining – but try telling that to Liverpool fans. What their incredible 5-4 win over Spanish side Alavés in the 2001 UEFA Cup meant was not just the conclusion of an incredible Treble of cup successes, but Anfield immortality for Frenchman Gérard Houllier.

Having already secured the League Cup earlier in the season, beating Birmingham, Liverpool were arguably tired out after their exertions in the FA Cup final against Arsenal the previous weekend; but to be run so close by the little Basque side made for a fantastic final for the neutrals. Two up through Markus Babbel and Steven Gerrard, 3-1 at half-time after man-of-the-match Gary McAllister's penalty, the Reds were pegged back time and time again, Jordi Cruyff of all people taking the game into added time.

The atmosphere in the steep-banked Westfalenstadion was just electric. This was a Liverpool team with plenty of home-grown players (Fowler, Owen, Murphy, Gerrard, Carragher), at the peak of its powers and always entertaining. So when McAllister's free-kick, with Alavés by now down to nine men, flicked off the head of Delfi Geli and into the net, it was more than ever a wonderful night to remember.

Liverpool players celebrate their unique cup Treble, thereby ending manager Gérard Houllier's three-year wait to bring silverware to Anfield in great style.

2001

Henman Flow Stemmed by the Rain

TIM HENMAN was just so British. Could any other nation have produced a professional sportsman so adept at being not quite good enough? The fact he was very popular made it even more desperate. Of Henman's six defeats in Grand Slam semi-finals, four came at Wimbledon in the space of five years, despite the backing of a huge crowd both on Centre Court and on Henman Hill.

The most agonising loss came in 2001, to Goran Ivanisevic. In the quarter-final, Henman had defeated a 19-year-old Swiss prodigy by the name of Roger Federer, who had in turn knocked out seven-times champion Pete Sampras – a changing of the guard, if ever there was one. This was surely Henman's chance; for once, it wasn't Sampras in the semi as it had been in both 1998 and 1999.

The match began on Friday, and after losing the first set, Henman was majestic. Battling out a second set tie-break, he went on to win the third set 6-0, in 15 minutes. Then came the rain and the jitters, and Ivanisevic, who had never beaten Tiger Tim, stormed back into the match. On Saturday, the Croat took the fourth set tie-break and was 3-2 up in the fifth on serve. More rain. On Sunday, the despondency really set in and the nail biting continued in earnest. At 4-3 down Henman double faulted to lose his service game, and Ivanisevic served it out. It was all over in a flash.

Tiger Tim was a tremendous player but watching him was a bitter-sweet experience as he so often snatched defeat from the jaws of victory.

TENNIS All England Lawn Tennis Championships
Men's Singles Final, Goran Ivanisevic v. Pat Rafter, Wimbledon, London, 10 July 2001

2001

Part Seven 2000–2011

Ivanisevic Wins the People's Wimbledon

Even though he beat Henman in the semi-final, Goran Ivanisevic was roared on to victory in the final by an unusual crowd, many of whom had queued up for two days and nights to get tickets.

WIMBLEDON HAS a reputation for being a bit stuffy. There's the price of the strawberries for a start and all those rules and regulations. So when the rain pushed the 2001 men's singles final into a third Monday, it was guaranteed to be different. It was the 'People's Final' – thousands could finally watch a game on Centre Court without spending a fortune – and, at the end of it, we got a People's Champion.

Goran Ivanisevic may have beaten Tim Henman in the semi-final but his was a wonderful story. The Croatian was in the championships thanks to a wild card. Three times previously he had reached the final, only for Andre Agassi and Pete Sampras, twice, to dash his hopes. The presence of Pat Rafter this time round guaranteed a big Australian contingent in the cheap seats, so Ivanisevic would have to keep his cool, which of course he couldn't.

It was his passion that endeared him to the fans, and it was writ large in an epic, five-set final, with the crowd roaring their approval of some brilliant and inspiring tennis. Ivanisevic really did play with his heart. And once he had achieved his lifetime dream, he could return home, to be greeted by another 150,000 people in Split.

Owen Sinks the Germans

Michael Owen celebrates the second goal of his famous hat-trick against Germany in Munich on a night when the pubs and clubs of England were packed with celebrating supporters … it doesn't often happen, but boy was that a sweet night!

BEATING THE Germans on their own patch: life surely doesn't get any better than that! Images of this match nestle sweetly in every England fan's memory of a night when everything simply came together. Of course it didn't seem that way when Carsten Jancker prodded the ball past David Seaman after only five minutes. Germany had won 1-0 at a rain-sodden Wembley in Kevin Keegan's final match as England manager, and here they were again.

But this was a different England and, after Michael Owen volleyed in Nicky Barmby's knock-down to make it 1-1, they simply tore the Germans apart. Steven Gerrard whistled one in from outside the area just before half-time, and Oliver Kahn was again left helpless by a classic Owen finish after the break. Gerrard put his Liverpool teammate in for his hat-trick and then even Emile Heskey got in on the act with a left-foot drive – 5-1!

It was unbelievable, almost surreal, with Sven-Göran Eriksson bathed in smiles on the Munich sidelines. Of course we should have known that it would not last, but isn't that what these kinds of moments are for?

Beckham's Redemption

THE MOST iconic footballer of his generation struck his most iconic pose when he rescued England from the perils of a World Cup play-off. The fact it was at Old Trafford, at the Stretford End, the fact that David Beckham was the captain and the sheer drama of the situation, the release of such tension, made it one of those jump-up-and-run-around-screaming moments.

A run of five straight victories in qualifying, including that famous 5-1 win over Germany in Munich, had left Sven-Göran Eriksson's team needing only to beat Greece at home in their final fixture. In fact, it turned out that Germany's draw with Finland meant one point would suffice, but no one knew that at the time. England had required second half substitute

Beckham played a captain's role that day: tackling, running, passing, and his efforts were rewarded with almost the final kick of the match, his free-kick sailing sweetly into Greece's net and taking England to the World Cup finals.

Teddy Sheringham to score with his first touch to equalise, only to fall behind again straight away.

Seconds remained when Sheringham was pushed in the back; free-kick 30 yards out. Beckham territory. The famous right foot, snug in its special England No. 7 boot emblazoned with the match date, swung. Perfection. Beckham sprinted off to the corner and, Christlike, saviour of the nation, bathed in the adulation. He would go on to purge himself too of sins against Argentina in Japan in the summer of 2002.

Rossi Wins the First of Five-in-a-Row

Valentino Rossi (left) glances across at his rival Max Biaggi. Rossi went on to win the British Grand Prix at Donington.

VALENTINO ROSSI was hardly an unknown when he captured the first of five straight world championship titles in 2001. We already knew that he was something special … and completely crazy.

In the final season of the 500cc era, Rossi toyed with his main rival Max Biaggi all year long, their spite for each other thinly disguised. At the opening race in Japan, Biaggi appeared to have tried to push Rossi into the dirt at 150mph. Two laps later Rossi passed Biaggi, finding time to flick the finger at him as he did so. The pair fought, literally, after the Catalan Grand Prix in June. Biaggi won, controversially, in Assen, with Rossi second and Loris Capirossi in third, fuming at his supposed Honda teammate for his dangerous tactics. But Rossi was setting his own rules, doing it his way. Then in practice for the British Grand Prix he crashed at 140mph, trashing his bike. Unperturbed, he took his place on the third row of the grid, and Donington was to see for the first time the familiar charge, the sensational speed. It was a brilliant win and was followed with an outlandish celebration.

The wins kept on coming, most thrillingly at Phillip Island in Australia, when Rossi as usual just would not accept defeat and conjured up a victory by 0.013 of a second. Two years later, he would defy a ten-second penalty to wipe out the opposition there. Rossi would go on to launch MotoGP into a new stratosphere. He was the self-styled king of the motorcycling world, and boy did we know it.

Curling on Top of the World

THE DESTINY of the 2002 Winter Olympic gold medal rested in skipper Rhona Martin's hand. But was this the Stone of Destiny? Or was she destined to fail? The next few seconds would tell. She and her teammates, Fiona MacDonald, Margaret Morton, Janice Rankin and Debbie Knox, had sacrificed an enormous amount – jobs, social life, family life – to represent Britain at the Games, and reaching the final had been no walk in the park. A promising start disintegrated and progression was taken out of their hands, but a Swiss victory over Germany gave them a lifeline. Victories over Sweden and then Germany took them to the semi-finals and an unexpected defeat of Canada. Now, with the scores tied 3-3 and the Swiss sitting in a protected, point-scoring position, Martin had one chance to steal the match and secure Britain's first

Winter Olympic gold for 18 years. She released her yellow stone. It evaded the red Swiss guard and bent towards its target. If it made inch-perfect contact with the red stone that lay kissing the inner circle, Martin and her team would be Olympic heroes. The slightest error, and the Swiss would take home gold. Contact was exact, Swiss hopes drifted away with their stone and the yellow of Britain sat proud, on the button, on top of the world. Back in the UK, the public collectively leapt from their sofas in unconfined happiness at victory in a sport few had even heard of days earlier. Simply marvellous.

It's on its way: Rhona Martin lets the Stone of Destiny go. Its course was true and Britain secured its first Winter Olympics gold medal since Torvill and Dean.

Lewis Masterclass Floors Tyson

Lennox Lewis lands a crunching right hand on Mike Tyson's face in the seventh round of their brutal fight in Memphis.

ANIMOSITY BETWEEN fighters is nothing new, but when it involves Mike Tyson it takes on extra proportions. After Lennox Lewis became the undisputed heavyweight champion of the world in 1997, Tyson sent him a message following his 38-second fight with Lou Savarese: 'I want to eat his children.'

Eighteen months later, the two held a press conference to announce Tyson's title challenge, but as Lewis emerged into the spotlight, Tyson went for him, punches were thrown and a brawl ensued. Tyson then turned his anger on the watching media, making obscene gestures and verbally abusing a female reporter. When the fight proper was eventually staged, to say it was highly anticipated is an understatement. The fact that it did not live up to its billing is testament to the quality of Lewis's boxing.

The West Ham-born champion controlled a sluggish-looking Tyson from the bell. By round seven, Lewis was using Tyson as a punch bag. In the eighth, an uppercut saw the American sag almost to his knees and take a standing count, before Lewis's right hand powered through Tyson's defence to land squarely on his chin and knock him out for the third time in his career. Lying on his back, with blood pouring from his eye and nose, 'Iron' Mike was out for the count. Lennox Lewis had confirmed himself as one of the all-time greats.

'Wayne Rooney – Remember the Name'

'ONCE A Blue, Always a Blue'. Well, Wayne Rooney may have gone back on that in many people's eyes when he took the Old Trafford shilling, but Everton fans were at least blessed with being present at the birth of a quite extraordinary football talent.

Rooney was still five days short of his 17th birthday when he announced himself to a world audience. Plenty already knew about the Croxteth-born phenomenon on home turf though; his goals had guided Everton to the FA Youth Cup final against Aston Villa the previous season, and he had already notched a couple at senior level, in the Worthington Cup against Wrexham.

But it was the context of Rooney's first Premier League goal, not least the dipping, swerving, rocket-like nature of his 25-yard strike past a flailing David Seaman, that was so spectacular. It brought Arsenal's incredible 30-match unbeaten run to an end. It came so late in the game that it made the Goodison stands shake. And Rooney, on as a substitute for only ten minutes, became the Premier League's youngest ever goalscorer, at least for a while. But perhaps most spectacular of all was the sheer look of this teenager – ridiculously strong for his age.

'Wayne Rooney – remember the name' said TV commentator Clive Tyldesley that evening as David Moyes no doubt wondered how long Everton would be able to hold on to their precious young talent.

Although he was not at Everton for long, Wayne Rooney's first Premiership goal, against Arsenal at Goodison, will remain long in the memories of those who witnessed it.

Jonny Comes Marching Home – With the Cup

THE ALL Blacks might have been pre-tournament favourites (again), but with an undefeated run of 14 matches (eventually broken only by France in a warm-up game), which included a Grand Slam and home and away victories over New Zealand and Australia, England arrived in Australia as the world's No. 1 team.

Confidence was high in the England camp, but although they continued to win, their group stage performances were not impressive. A quarter-final encounter with a resurgent Wales saw England's dream in serious jeopardy. They were 10-3 down at half-time and struggling. In the dressing-room, coach Clive Woodward acted decisively, bringing Mike Catt on for Dan Luger, and captain Martin

Jonny Wilkinson completes his *Boys' Own* story as he lets fly with the most famous drop-goal of England's rugby history.

Johnson roused his troops with a powerful speech. Catt's entrance proved to be the turning point of England's tournament, transforming a misfiring Jonny Wilkinson. His kicks plus a Will Greenwood try saw England home 28-17.

Next up, France in the rain. A converted Betsen try gave Les Bleus an early lead, but that was the sum total of the French resistance. Jonny kicked them firmly into touch, landing all of England's points in a 24-7 victory. The bandwagon was now really rolling.

In a pulsating and incredibly tense World Cup final, Australia twice clawed themselves back from

'He drops for World Cup glory. It's up! It's over! He's done it!'

defeat. Having been 14-5 up at half-time, England failed to score a point in the second half and, with the last kick of the ball in the regulation 80 minutes, Elton Flatley forced extra time. Another Wilkinson penalty and another nerveless Flatley kick with less than two minutes of the match remaining once again brought Australia level, 17-17.

England had one chance left. A successful line-out was followed by a blistering 20-metre burst from Matt Dawson. But it left the scrum-half out of position. Enter Martin Johnson. Demonstrating incredible courage and immense leadership, the captain chose to go one more time at the Australian defence, risking the ball being ripped from his grasp, to allow Dawson to return to his station. It

Captain Martin Johnson holds up the Webb Ellis Trophy (top) – a triumph that led to unprecedented scenes of jubilation as crowds lined the streets of London to welcome home the victorious players.

works: from a ruck the ball is successfully funnelled back to Dawson. Ian Robertson takes up the story: 'There's 35 seconds to go, this is the one. It's coming back to Jonny Wilkinson. He drops for World Cup glory. It's up! It's over! He's done it!' Classic radio commentary that sums up the moment beautifully.

The Wallabies have one final play. Trevor Woodman makes a magnificent catch, the ball is fed to Mike Catt, who kicks to touch – the whistle goes, 20-17 to England. World Champions, thanks to the most famous drop-goal in history.

'You Win Some; You Draw Some'

LEICESTER'S PAUL Dickov almost spoiled the party with a first-half goal, but after Thierry Henry's penalty and Patrick Vieira had given Arsenal their final victory of the Premiership campaign, the festivities could begin – 26 wins, 12 draws, 0 defeats. The Invincibles were born (Preston could now be consigned to history) and Arsène Wenger's side had pulled off one of sport's most extraordinary achievements – an unbeaten season. And they did it in brilliant style.

Henry's 30 goals were obviously pivotal, the Frenchman at his absolute unstoppable best, but all over the field the Gunners played divine football. Dennis Bergkamp and Robert Pires (who himself scored 14 times)

Arsenal players celebrate with the Premiership trophy – the spoils from their incredible unbeaten season.

pulled the strings, with Vieira a colossus alongside Gilberto Silva in midfield. Jens Lehmann, a surprise signing the previous summer, could take much of the credit for only 26 goals conceded, but an almost ever-present back four of Lauren, Kolo Touré, Sol Campbell and Ashley Cole were clearly crucial in an undefeated campaign.

Arsenal rode their luck at times, but also battled back from adversity after cup defeats to Manchester United and Chelsea. It was a phenomenal season. And the icing on the cake? They clinched the title at White Hart Lane.

Wasps Refuse to Lie Down

ENGLISH FOOTBALL has taken a hell of a beating twice. Once by the Norwegians in 1981 and the second time in 2003-04, when England won the Rugby World Cup and rugby stood up to its bigger brother and knocked it flat. The arrogant sibling may not have stayed down for long, but during that season the oval-ball sport proved it was no longer cowed by the riches of the round ball.

At the centre of it all was Lawrence Dallaglio. From playing every minute of England's World Cup triumph, Dallaglio then led his Wasps teammates on a glorious odyssey. Their Heineken Cup pool match in Perpignan typified the colour and brutality of the club game, the 34-6 scoreline belying the intensity of the occasion. The Munster semi-final at Lansdowne Road was all passion, with 51,000 fans watching the lead fluctuate throughout the match. With ten minutes to go, Wasps were ten points down but pulled level, before Trevor Leota just managed to ground the ball and the London side were in their first European final, against Toulouse.

Here was the drama. Wasps 20-11 up midway through the second half, Dallaglio sin-binned, and suddenly it's 20-20. With seconds remaining, Rob Howley sends a grubber kick down the line. Full-back Clement Poitrenaud shepherds it closely, but it doesn't bounce out, instead flipping awkwardly but beautifully for Howley to score. A week later, Bath felt the Wasps sting in the Premiership final and a fabulous season came to an end for the London side.

Lawrence Dallaglio (with the Heineken Cup) takes centre stage as he had done throughout the 2003-04 season, leading Wasps to a cup and Premiership Double.

Paula Radcliffe's Tears

THE EVENING of 22 August 2004 on the streets of Athens was meant to be when Paula Radcliffe put to rest the tag of 'gallant loser', having missed out on medals in the Atlanta and Sydney Olympics. Since those 2000 Games, Radcliffe had won Commonwealth 5,000 gold, European 10,000 gold, plus two London marathons, the second in a new world record. But, then and there, the Olympics was all that mattered.

In hot, humid conditions, Radcliffe starts well, but after an hour her head begins to bob and she seems to be hurting. At 16 miles, the Japanese runner Noguchi quickens and Radcliffe struggles to respond, dropping back to fourth place. At 19 miles she fights back, moving bravely up to second, but the challenge is unsustainable. Three miles to go and with supporters lining the street

Some athletes produce an emotional response: Paula Radcliffe is one of those, and perhaps never more so than when she broke down 3 miles from the finish of the Olympic marathon in Athens.

and many more in the stadium watching events on screen, Radcliffe knows she has nothing left and staggers to a halt. In distress, in agony, she collapses by the side of the road, head in hands, devastated and in tears.

To some it is a case of quitting. Injury and a negative reaction to anti-inflammatory drugs are later suspected, but the reasons hardly matter. Sport is both kind and cruel; it is how you react that counts. Radcliffe faced the world with dignity, attempted to make amends in the 10,000 metres and went on to become the greatest female marathon runner of all time. She let no one down on that evening in Athens.

Emms and Robertson's Silver Lining

YOU NEED 20-20 vision, agility, strength and fitness to be a world-class badminton player. With the shuttlecock flying back and forth at incredible speed, then dropping suddenly short, to be dinked long again, then smashed hard into the corner, with barely a second to react and make shot selections, you must also be able to trust your instincts. And that is just in singles. In doubles there is an added element of unpredictability – your partner. Add telepathy to the list.

Fortunately, the British duo of Nathan Robertson and Gail Emms had the full set, and in Athens in 2004 it all came together magnificently. Having seen off German, Chinese and Danish challenges, they faced the defending champions, the Chinese pair Gao Ling and Zhang Jun in what turned out to be a nail-biting finale.

Unceremoniously swatted away in the first game, 15-1, the Britons came out fighting for the second, taking it 15-12. They looked on course for a stunning victory after coming back from 3-0 down in the third to lead 7-3. But the Chinese pair proved to just have the edge, and took the game 15-12 and with it the gold medal. Although disappointing, it was a fantastic run by Robertson and Emms that captured the imagination of the British public. They were rewarded two years later when the pair went one step further in the World Championships, making their newfound fans very happy indeed.

With all senses firing Gail Emms and Nathan Robertson's fantastic performance in the Olympic badminton doubles in Athens earned them a well-deserved silver medal.

Kelly Holmes at the Double

Head steady, eye focused, arms and legs pumping powerfully ...

THE DOUBLE. In every sport it has a special allure. In athletics, while there are other contenders, surely the magical combination is the Olympic 800 and 1,500 metres. Less than a week before the 2004 Games, Kelly Holmes decided she would launch a bid to scale Mount Olympus and seek the fabled prize. Entering the 800 metres was a risk, given Holmes' injury-stricken past. But in Athens, for almost the first time in her career, she had arrived fully fit at a major championship.

At 34 years old, having recovered from clinical depression and a period of self-harming, it was now or never. Off the bend in the 800 metres, there was a lot to do. World champion Maria Mutola was kicking on strongly. Head steady, eye focused, arms and legs pumping powerfully, Holmes drew her training partner in, centimetre

After winning the 800 metres, and lapping up the glory (above), Kelly Holmes wanted more … and she got it five days later, streaking home to double gold in the 1,500 metres (opposite).

by centimetre, overtaking her and keeping just ahead of the fast-closing Benhassi and Ceplak on the line. Unable to quite believe it, she stared at the stadium screen for confirmation. When it came, the smile and the eyes said it all.

Five days later she had to do it all again in her preferred event, the 1,500 metres. Running the perfect race, she took the lead in the home straight, powering past Tomashova of Russia to complete Britain's greatest achievement in athletics. Holmes became the first British woman to win two Olympic golds at the same Games and the country's first athlete since Albert Hill in 1920 to achieve the Double. Incredible.

Khan Steps Up to the Plate

ATHENS 2004 was always going to be quite some Olympics. The return to the spiritual home of the Games after so long guaranteed not only a sense of occasion, nicely reflected in touches like the wreaths given to medal-winners, but also an extra level of determination to succeed. Not that Amir Khan needed it.

The 17-year-old lightweight from Bolton was nothing if not confident – but then if you are the only member of Team GB's boxing contingent, and going up against someone like Mario Kindelan for a gold medal, that tends to help. Khan was phenomenal on his way to the final, with the speed of his punches just too much even for experienced opponents: first a home fighter,

Amir Khan (left) launched his boxing career at the Athens Olympics, outfighting everyone on his way to the final. He came close, very close, but Cuba's reigning Olympic champion Mario Kindelan (right) proved one step too far.

next the European champion. Kindelan proved a step too far – the Cuban was almost twice Khan's age, reigning Olympic champion and world champion – but the teenager got so close.

The backing Khan received was extraordinary, with his family becoming stars in their own right, a huge crowd watching back home at the Bolton Arena and the nation cheering him on. It was a major turning point in British sport: with many of Khan's fellow Muslims draped in the Union Jack. Khan did us all proud.

The Tanni Grey-Thompson Phenomenon

INSPIRATIONAL. DEDICATED. Obsessive. Determined. All words that go some way towards explaining the phenomenal success of Tanni Grey-Thompson. Never were they more in evidence than in the Paralympic 100 metres in Athens.

With the weight of personal, team and national expectations resting on her shoulders for her first race of the Games, the 800 metres, Grey-Thompson had crumbled. Allowing herself to become boxed in, she finished seventh and was devastated, to the point that Team GB gave her the option to return home. But that is not her style; that is not the attitude that has won her an unprecedented haul of medals; that is not the way of Britain's greatest ever disabled athlete.

Three days later, shaking with nerves, she lined up for the sprint. A poor start did not faze her. She was focused, and with Grey-Thompson that equates to a powerful weapon. Just over halfway down the track, she hit the front, coming home in the best time of her life, 17.24 seconds. The spectre of failure had been exorcised. She repeated the trick in the 400 metres, setting a new Games record.

Without even mentioning the European and world titles, the statistics of Grey-Thompson's career almost defy belief: five Paralympic Games, winning 16 medals, including 11 golds; 6 London Marathon victories; and over 30 world records. Now a baroness and a life peer, any slackers in the House of Lords had better shape up.

Tanni Grey-Thompson showed all the attributes that have made her such a magnificent Olympian in winning gold in the Paralympic 100 metres in Athens.

GB Slay the US Dragon

VICTORIES OVER the USA are always sweet and it was in the sport of wheelchair basketball that one of Britain's greatest triumphs came. The sport had first grabbed a share of the limelight at the Sydney Paralympics, when a bronze medal eluded GB at the buzzer, but in Athens four years later we finally had our podium place.

Britain had been one of the favourites going into the competition, but disappointed in the group stage, leading to a tough quarter-final match against the Americans, who had won bronze in 2000. With memories of defeat burning bright, GB were never behind this time round. But with less than 20 seconds remaining, the USA drew level. It was Ade Adepitan's time to shine. Drawing a foul, the guard coolly slotted his free throws, and a semi-final was assured. It was a momentous victory, which GB could not repeat against the Australians; but when the Netherlands were crushed in the play-off, we had bronze.

It was Britain's 94th medal of another superb Paralympics, and those wheelchair basketball players had taken the game to the mainstream. It emerged later that the Games weren't even shown live in the USA. In 2012, Adepitan will be broadcasting from his home city.

Great Britain's Ade Adepitan (right) draws a last-minute foul from the USA's Jeff Glasbrenner, before slotting home the resulting free throws to seal a momentous quarter-final victory.

Rebirth of the Welsh Rugby Nation

SPEED, STRENGTH, flair and fighting spirit. The Grand Slam-winning Wales team of 2005 had it all, and were crafted by Mike Ruddock from wooden spooners of two years previously into a team that played attacking rugby at its most exhilarating. The Six Nations that year produced some thrilling encounters – as long as Wales were playing.

England at the Millennium Stadium for the opening salvo: Shane Williams as ever the tormentor of the English defence, then Gavin Henson with a monster penalty to send the home crowd wild. The poster boy for the Wales team, mocked for his grooming but at his peak as a player (and celebrity), Henson had earlier demolished Matthew Tait on the England centre's debut. Henson was immense. In Paris, run ragged

Gavin Henson played a major part in Wales' triumphant Grand Slam-winning season in 2005. He has rarely hit such heights again.

by half-time and without injured skipper Gareth Thomas, it was Martyn Williams, the player of the championship, who inspired a momentous comeback with two tries. Stephen Jones, metronomic with the boot, sealed the victory. Then back in Cardiff, where Ireland hadn't lost since 1983, nerves jangling, but from Gethin Jenkins' charge-down try there was only ever going to be one winner.

A sea of red, Thomas and Michael Owen lifting the trophy – 11 years since the last one, a first Grand Slam for 27 years! Cue bedlam. Wales were wonderful and worthy winners.

Mourinho Delivers

'PLEASE DON'T call me arrogant but I'm European champion and I think I'm a special one.' It was some way to introduce yourself to the British press, and was the first of many sound bites that would make José Mourinho a tabloid darling.

Porto's achievement in winning the Champions League (and the UEFA Cup) was astonishing, but Mourinho would have been nothing (despite the pose, the clothes, the salt-and-pepper hair) had he not delivered at Chelsea. And he was the Special One, the alchemist who could turn Roman Abramovich's millions into Premier League gold – a first league title for the Blues in 50 years.

Claudio Ranieri had done much of the groundwork – Petr Cech and Claude Makelele were crucial to the defensive mastery that helped Chelsea to the top. But the team was transformed in the summer of 2004 by the arrival of Didier Drogba and Arjen Robben and Portuguese defenders Ricardo Carvalho and Paulo Ferreira. Frank Lampard's goals and the captaincy of John Terry were also central to their success.

Six points clear at the top of the Premiership at Christmas, they won the League Cup in March and by April, following a 2-0 win at Bolton, they were champions with a record 95 points. It was Mourinho who blended them into winners, who made them a team, who was, as he himself proclaimed, 'a top manager'.

You can't argue with that … José Mourinho arrived at Chelsea in the summer of 2004; nine months later the club had won the league championship for the first time since 1955.

Motherwell Win Title ... for Rangers

Rangers celebrate on the Easter Road pitch after Celtic's defeat at Motherwell had consigned the Hoops to the runners-up spot.

ON THE last day of a glorious season, Celtic travelled to Motherwell knowing a win would secure them the league title. Rangers, two points behind but with a better goal difference, made their way along the M8 to Edinburgh and Easter Road, with the faintest of hopes that miracles do sometimes happen. But surely not today? A good Hibs side were lying third in the table, while injury-hit Motherwell limped 47 points behind Celtic.

After 88 minutes, with both Glasgow sides leading their respective matches 1-0, the helicopter transporting the Premier League trophy was skimming across the summer sky towards Fir Park. The 'Gers fans, ears pressed against their radios, had all but given up hope of that miracle. But then a mishit shot just outside the edge of the

Celtic penalty box fell to Scott McDonald. He controlled the ball on his chest, and hooked it over his left shoulder and into the top corner of the net. As the Motherwell fans celebrated, they could almost hear the roar from Easter Road. The helicopter hovered in midflight.

Two minutes into injury time, with Martin O'Neill's players shattered, McDonald repeated the trick, this time looping a shot over the Celtic keeper. By then, the helicopter had Arthur's Seat well and truly in its sights. Rangers had won their 51st league title in the most dramatic fashion.

The Miracle of Istanbul

Liverpool players rejoice with the Champions League trophy after the game of two halves to end them all.

IN THE first half of the 2005 Champions League final against Milan, Liverpool did not merely walk through a storm; they stood in the full force of a tornado. Facing a side featuring seven players who had won the trophy two years previously, augmented by Jaap Stam, Kaká, Cafu and Hernán Crespo, the Merseysiders were outclassed.

Paolo Maldini's strike after 50 seconds, a goal-line clearance from Luis García, a borderline offside against Andriy Shevchenko and two wonderfully worked goals from Crespo told the story. Liverpool were denied a penalty, but it seemed that it would matter little. At 3-0 down, humiliation limitation was their only realistic ambition. Some Liverpool fans were seen leaving the stadium for the long walk back to town.

During the break, somehow, Rafa Benitez lifted his players' heads, altered his tactics to stifle Kaká and left the rest to Steven Gerrard. A towering header gave Liverpool hope and the captain's exhortations both to fans and players produced an incredible six minutes that saw the Reds draw level through Vladimir Smicer and Xabi Alonso.

The hero's baton was then handed to Jerzy Dudek, who had saved brilliantly just before Gerrard scored but had been prone to errors throughout the match. A barely believable double save from Shevchenko ensured penalties. Arms waving, Dudek bounced on his line, occasionally stepped off it and watched Serginho blast over, saved well from Andrea Pirlo and again denied Shevchenko to seal Milan's fate. Miracles really can happen. How those fans who left at half-time can forgive themselves... well, who knows?

Hatton's Big Fight Night

MANCHESTER HAD never seen anything quite like it. A 2 a.m. fight (well, the city had seen a few of those), with a packed MEN Arena baying for blood and for the triumph of their native son. An IBF light welterweight world title belt was at stake, but there was much, much more to it than that. Ricky Hatton, pride of Manchester, in the colours of his beloved City, was a massive underdog against Kostya Tszyu, the Russian-born Australian, ten years a world champion and a man with a fearsome right hand. The Hitman knew he was going to take some punishment.

Round after round he stuck at his task, getting on the inside, ducking and diving, absorbing the beating, and always hitting back, attacking. As the fight wore on, the 35-year-old Tszyu would surely tire. When he needed to,

Hatton wrestled and brawled. There were low punches; it got ugly. And still the fight went on, the crowd in a frenzy, the Hitman increasingly putting his opponent on the ropes. Then, astonishingly, after an 11th round when Hatton again threw everything he had at him, Tszyu could take no more.

Manchester roared. Ricky Hatton had stepped up to the big time. A man of the people, and now a champion, with an army of fans who would follow him wherever he went. Of course, eventually, Hatton's force, his domination, would wane. But let's remember him for those big fight nights.

Ouch! Kostya Tszyu takes a Hatton right-hander on the chin as the Hitman lives up to his name during one of the finest performances of his career.

London Awarded 2012 Olympics

David Beckham and Sir Stephen Redgrave embrace after the announcement of London's successful bid to host the 2012 Olympic Games.

IN HIS opening remarks to the International Olympic Committee (IOC), Seb Coe explained London's vision for the 2012 Olympics was to 'reach young people all around the world, to connect them with the inspirational power of the Games so that they are inspired to choose sport'. He ended with, 'On behalf of the young of today, the athletes of tomorrow and the Olympians of the future, we humbly submit the bid of London 2012.'

Over an inspiring 45 minutes, the presentation featured HRH The Princess Royal, British Olympic Committee chairman Craig Reedie, Mayor Ken Livingstone, Olympic champion Denise Lewis, Olympic Minister Tessa Jowell, and a message from Tony Blair, interspersed with a film of four youngsters inspired to take up sport after watching the 2012 Games in London on television. Until that moment, Paris had been favourite ... suddenly it wasn't so clear-cut. Three rounds of secret voting saw Moscow, New York and Madrid drop out. The final round was incredibly close, 54 to 50 as it turned out.

IOC president Jacques Rogge stood up. 'The International Olympic Committee has the honour of announcing that the Games of the Thirtieth Olympiad in 2012 are awarded to the city of ... London.' Cue cheers, hugs and tears from the huge crowds gathered in Trafalgar Square and Stratford, but most of all from the fawn-suited and blue-shirted British bid team in the room itself. They had every right to be pleased.

England's Women Throw Down the Gauntlet

WHAT A glorious Ashes summer 2005 was. Heroes lauded at the open-top bus parade through the streets of London. Clare Connor, Charlotte Edwards, Katherine Brunt, Jenny Gunn, Arran Brindle, Isa Guha … Yes, let's not forget that the England Women's Cricket team pulled off an astonishing achievement of their own, one that even put the feats of the men's side into perspective. A first Ashes triumph for 42 years! Following a drawn First Test at Hove, they beat Australia in the decider at an extremely damp New Road ground at Worcester. Their first Test victory over the Aussies for 21 years.

Brunt was at the forefront of a first innings that saw the Aussies skittled for just 131, with her maiden five-wicket haul. The Barnsley bowler then showed what she could do with the bat, striking a debut half-century in a vital last-wicket partnership with Guha, after Jenny Gunn, Connor and Claire Taylor had laid the foundations for an England total of 289.

Brunt got another four victims in the second innings. England required just 75 for victory. At 1 for 2 though, the nerves were as exposed as could be. Connor and Edwards, captain and vice-captain, restored confidence. The winning runs came from Brindle just before tea with an outpouring of joy.

The team would be paraded at the Oval a few days later, inspiring Michael Vaughan's team maybe. They even got to share the prime minister's garden for a while (if not, one senses, quite the same quantity of refreshments).

England's Jenny Gunn celebrates taking the wicket of Aussie captain Belinda Clarke in the First Test at Hove.

England's Ashes Victory

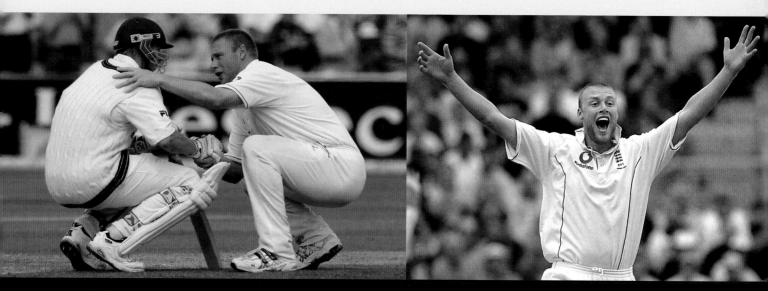

With Freddie rampant, the Aussies' number was surely up.

WELL, AT least the man of the series award was easy. It was Flintoff's Ashes, even if Michael Vaughan got the captain's credit. It was epic; the series swung one way then the other in the most agonising fashion. It dominated the summer, and not much work was done when it was on. The bare facts say that England won 2-1 in 2005, winning the Ashes for the first time since 1987 (even though it felt a lot longer).

Australia, Glenn McGrath in particular, had destroyed England at Lord's – the traditional start to a Test series in England. However, McGrath's absence for the Second Test at Edgbaston was quite another matter, and this was a match that should be required viewing for anyone who thinks cricket is boring. It was a rollercoaster ride, unbearable to watch at times, and ended in the closest Ashes

Freddie Flintoff personified the most compelling Ashes series for years – during the thrilling Second Test his aggressive bowling illustrated the intense rivalry between the teams but did not prevent him sharing the agony of defeat with Brett Lee (left).

match ever. England's batsmen responded by gaining a 100-run lead in the first innings, but second time around Shane Warne bamboozled them again, Andrew Strauss in particular. Only Andrew Flintoff was able to respond, with an immense innings, including a six over the stand. Australia needed 280 odd to win, but at 175 for 8, with Freddie rampant, the Aussies' number was surely up. Shane Warne bludgeoned his way to 42, but Flintoff got him too.

Still 60 needed – no chance. But Brett Lee and the last man, Michael Kasprowicz, edged closer and closer. England made it easier: a dropped

Flintoff's all-round brilliance and insane strength saved the series at Edgbaston.

After the drawn Third Test at Old Trafford, England captain Michael Vaughan called his team together for a huddle. 'Look,' he said, 'See how happy they are just to draw a game against us.' Suitably inspired, England won the next Test by three wickets.

The England players were apparently astonished when thousands of flag-waving cricket lovers turned out to greet their new heroes on the now-obligatory open-topped bus parade around London, which ended, for some, in the fountains at Trafalgar Square.

catch, four byes. It would have been a disastrous defeat, certainly the end of the Ashes. But then at the last gasp, just two runs behind, Kasprowicz was caught behind off Harmison.
It was pandemonium.

And it stayed like that until the end. It went down to the last wicket again at Old Trafford, but Brett Lee, with McGrath this time, hung on for the draw. England almost blew it at Trent Bridge, but the unlikely figure of Ashley Giles hit the winning runs. Then Kevin Pietersen emerged to take the plaudits at the Oval, in partnership with Giles, and the weather did the rest: rain at last.

If Glenn McGrath had been fit for all five Tests, could England have done it? Shane Warne took 40 wickets in the series; the opening bowler would have fancied getting just as many. England had no answer for McGrath at Lord's. Only Flintoff's all-round brilliance and insane strength saved the series at Edgbaston. But that was all ifs and buts – as it was the nation went mad. London came to a standstill and the players got plastered. It was a wonderful summer of cricket.

Ronaldo is a Winker

IF THERE is anything worse than England losing in a penalty shootout, then it is England losing in a penalty shootout to Portugal with Cristiano Ronaldo scoring the winning penalty, the Ronaldo who has just got Wayne Rooney sent off. Football-wise, it's worse than anything Germany have ever inflicted on us.

Of all the World Cup disappointments, this quarter-final exit in Gelsenkirchen after a 0-0 draw and a 3-1 defeat in the shootout, had the added component of incredulity (not Portugal again, not after the raw wounds of Euro 2004!) spiced with hate. Yes, Rooney left his foot in clumsily on Ricardo Carvalho who, if not in Ronaldo's league when it comes to acting, can still writhe like the best. Yet referee Horacio Elizondo (an Argentinian, just for fun) could have let it go, let the game be decided

In a show of splendid choreography, Portugal's Petit (No. 8) and Ronaldo gesture dramatically at the wounded Carvalho at their feet. It worked, Rooney was off, Ronaldo winked and proved that we were right about him all along. Oh yes, and England lost on penalties … again.

mano a mano, were it not for the pleading of the Portuguese players.

Ronaldo, of course, was the worst culprit, the prime whinger. His Manchester United teammates – not just Rooney, but Rio Ferdinand and Gary Neville – could not believe what they had witnessed. After the debacle was over, Ronaldo would return to Old Trafford, would win the Premier League, then the Champions League and would be booed wherever he played in England.

When Portugal lost their World Cup semi-final to France (thanks to a Zidane penalty), there were cheers as he was reduced to tears.

Zidane's Had Enough

SOMETIMES MOMENTS are unforgettable because they are just so unexpected. And who could have predicted how Zinedine Zidane would choose to end his football career? Because doesn't it now seem as though he chose to go out that way, the ultimate expression of 'OK, I've had enough'?

Sport can inflict all kinds of stresses and strains on its participants. Walking away from it can be hard. Best to make it 100 per cent final. Burn those bridges to the ground. The finest footballer of his generation will no longer be remembered just for the phenomenal skills, vision and balance; the trophies with Juventus and Real Madrid; his status as an icon of the new French society; his two headers in the 1998 World Cup final as France thumped Brazil in Paris; his penalty chipped past Gianluigi Buffon

What a way to go: Zinedine Zidane, one of the finest footballers the world has ever seen, gets his marching orders after being goaded into retaliation by Italy's Marco Materazzi.

to open the scoring in Berlin eight years later; his brilliance against Brazil in the quarter-final, the last time, it seemed, that he really enjoyed playing football. No, added to the memories now will be his headbutt to the chest of Marco Materazzi, when football was no fun any more.

It was as if Zidane the immortal had decided to return to the realm of the human, brought down to earth by a normal, mortal Italian defender. The world watched, aghast, as the incident was replayed time and time again, with the World Cup winding to a close and victory on penalties for Italy – Zidane, the god of football, was walking away from the game for ever.

Tiger's Tears

GOLF, LET'S face it, is not the most emotional of sports – with the obvious exception of the Ryder Cup. But to play the game, with its extraordinary demands of consistency and control, when all seems to be falling apart around you, is a feat that requires the deepest strength.

Back in 2006, Tiger Woods was out on his own as world No. 1. He was defending champion at the Open in July, but back in May, his father and sporting inspiration, Earl Woods, had passed away. At his first event back on tour, the US Open, Tiger missed the cut. Unthinkable. His bereavement was clearly affecting his game. But on the sun-baked fairways of the Royal Liverpool, Tiger's genius held firm, and he led the field

It's hard to know whether Tiger's tears were of joy for his victory or sadness for the recent loss of his dad. In retrospect it's possible to suggest that he should have saved them for the storm that was to come later in his career.

almost from the start, opening with brilliant rounds of 67 and 65.

The challenges of Sergio Garcia, Ernie Els, and Chris DiMarco – who, poignantly, had recently lost his own mother – were brushed off. A final putt on the 18th sealed a two-shot victory, back-to-back triumphs in the Open and an 11th Major, but a first without his father. Woods' caddie, Steve Williams, could only offer an arm around the shoulder as the grief poured out of the golfer. You could not fail to be moved.

Darren Clarke's Triumph Over Tragedy

THE PRESSURES of the Ryder Cup are enough, without playing when you've just lost your wife. It was achievement enough for Darren Clarke to step out at the K Club in 2006. For him then to collect maximum points as Europe won the trophy for an unprecedented third time went beyond the limits of emotional bravery.

In normal circumstances, the Northern Irishman would have been a shoe-in for his fifth consecutive appearance, but the clash came just six weeks after Heather Clarke lost her battle against breast cancer. Clarke declared himself available for selection. Ian Woosnam picked him as a wild card. And with the Irish galleries behind their man like never before, Clarke was sublime, ever the fierce competitor.

His partnership with Lee Westwood, as at Oakland Hills two years previously, was unbeatable. First Phil Mickelson and Chris DiMarco, then Tiger Woods and Jim Furyk succumbed in the four-balls. For the singles, even with a healthy lead, Clarke was in a pivotal position. No matter – Zach Johnson was dispatched 3 & 2, Clarke raised his arms in triumph, Europe romped to victory and there was not a dry eye in the house. How Zara Phillips won the BBC Sports Personality of the Year award over Clarke in 2006 still stretches the bounds of credulity.

One of Heather Clarke's final wishes was for her husband Darren to play in the Ryder Cup in Ireland. He granted her wish, courtesy of captain Ian Woosnam, and played brilliantly, winning maximum points from his match-ups. After the tournament he retreated to grieve, only returning to the sport 15 months later. A brave man indeed.

Sport at Its Best

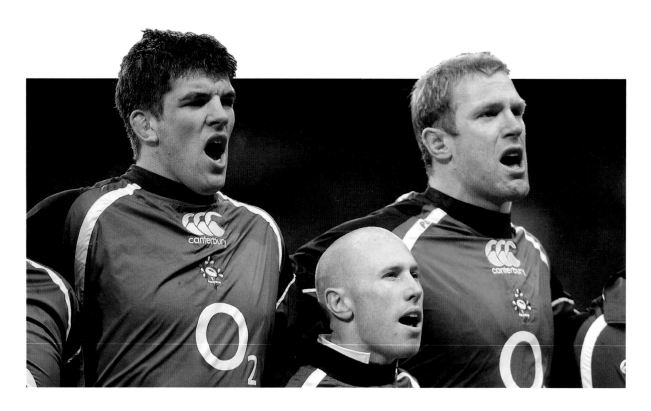

Irish players belt out the Irish anthems as a glorious sing-along heralds the end of 87 years of Anglo-Irish tension about the Croke Park massacre – the original Bloody Sunday.

SPORT has the capacity to move, excite, unify, surprise, and deliver extraordinary moments that show the very best in people. This capacity has never been better displayed than at Croke Park in 2007. It is hard to overestimate the poignancy or significance of this game. On 21 November 1920, in an act of brutal revenge, British Black and Tan forces opened fire on the crowd gathered in Croke Park to watch a Gaelic football match between Dublin and Tipperary. Thirteen fans and one Tipperary player, Michael Hogan, were killed. Many more were injured. Under the rules of the Gaelic Athletic Association, rugby and soccer were banned from the ground, but this restriction was temporarily lifted in 2005 while Lansdowne Road was redeveloped. Following Ireland's match against France two weeks earlier, the visit by

England was only the second rugby match to be played in the stadium. Thoughts inevitably turned to 1920 and focused on whether it was appropriate to play 'God Save the Queen'. The decision was taken to proceed, and as the band struck up and the English players sang, the predominantly Irish crowd showed huge respect. As the last note died, the crowd applauded vigorously. And then emotion and national pride erupted in a glorious display of singing to the Irish anthems of 'The Soldier's Song' and 'Ireland's Call'. As for the rugby, perhaps fittingly Ireland rampaged their way to their biggest win ever over England, 43-13. This was sport at its best.

Arsenal Ladies' Unique Feat

THE MOST successful football team of a generation. At one stage they won 51 consecutive games before being held to a 0-0 draw by Everton. They were the first British club to be crowned European champions. And yet they struggled to gain mainstream attention for a quite exceptional record.

The Arsenal Ladies team, put together by Vic Akers in 1987, has rewritten the history books. Thirty-two major trophies, from 2000 onwards, virtually unbeatable in league and cup. And in 2007 came ultimate achievement: Premier League, FA Cup, Premier League Cup and European Cup. (Oh, and on top of that they won the FA Women's Community Shield as well as the local London County FA Women's Cup – that's every single competition available to them, earning a unique Sextuple!) Take that, Manchester United.

The UEFA Women's Cup triumph was phenomenal – no club outside Germany or Scandinavia had won it before (or since). Arsenal's opponents in the final, Umea, were fully professional, boasting the likes of the Brazilian Marta and Hanna Ljungberg. And the Gunners were without their star forward, Kelly Smith. But after Alex Scott had scored a sensational long-distance, injury-time away goal in Sweden, Akers' team repelled everything thrown at them in the second leg. Emma Byrne in goal was again outstanding. Karen Carney and Katie Chapman fought for everything. Anita Asante and captain Jayne Ludlow lifted the trophy. And for these Invincibles, their feat will surely remain unique.

Joy unconfined for the Arsenal Ladies as they celebrate their UEFA Women's Cup triumph over Swedish club Umea.

2008

JT Slips Up

John Terry is a portrait of utter desolation after missing what would have been a Champions League-winning penalty.

IT WAS a horrible night. Not a horrible night if you're a Manchester United fan, of course. They won the Champions League for a second time and were kings of Europe for a third. It was a horrible night of torrential rain in Moscow, not the most ideal destination for an all-English cup final anyway. The match was played in difficult conditions on a sodden and just-relaid pitch. Careful now!

Losing your standing foot when taking a penalty is a fate that has befallen many players: David Beckham, notoriously, in a World Cup qualifier in Istanbul – and the ground would cave in for him again at Euro 2004. We're not the best at pressure spot-kicks anyway, are we? But to hit the post from 12 yards when your club's first ever Champions League is on the line, in your first final, when you're captain, when the world

outside Chelsea is willing you to miss? Poor old John Terry …

Perhaps the fates were on United's side. Fifty years since Munich and all that; it was Bobby Charlton's night as much as Paul Scholes'. The match had finished 1-1 after extra time, with an abundance of chances at both ends, but Didier Drogba's red card deprived Avram Grant's side of a talismanic figure (and fifth penalty-taker). Still, Ronaldo (again to the neutrals' delight) was first to crack in the shootout. All Terry had to do was score.

Edwin van der Sar's save from Nicolas Anelka won the trophy … but try telling that to the Chelsea skipper.

2008

Part Seven 2000–2011

The Finest Final?

WAS IT the greatest Wimbledon final ever? It deserves serious consideration. Naysayers suggest Roger Federer had already reached the summit and was meandering down the other side. His defeat to Rafael Nadal at the French Open a month previously, when he won only four games, offers ammunition. But Federer's epic match against Andy Roddick 12 months later, to lift his 15th Grand Slam trophy, suggests otherwise.

The weather switched between sunshine and rain and reflected the contrasting styles – Nadal all speed, aggression, power and grit, Federer the sublimely gifted craftsman with underlying steel. Nadal broke in the third game and held on for the set. At 4-1 in the second, the Swiss player looked certain to level, but Nadal turned up the heat to take it 6-4. At 3-3 and 0-40 down in the third, Federer looked finished, but showed his mettle and saved the game. The subsequent rain delay served him better.

Federer went on to win the set on a tie-break and saved two match points in the fourth, the second with a stunning backhand down the line with no backlift, to take that tie-break 10-8. With darkness falling, the fifth went with serve until the 15th game. Nadal broke and then incredibly – almost as if the tennis gods didn't want the match to end – three championship points went begging before Federer's forehand hit the net, leaving Nadal to collapse in joy.

Resilience over guile? Perhaps. Federer had 13 chances to break; he converted only one, but it made for breathtaking tennis.

Rafael Nadal held off an incredible fightback by Roger Federer to win his first Wimbledon title and end the Swiss star's five-year reign at the All England Club.

Harrington Does it Again

IF PÁDRAIG Harrington's 2007 Open Championship was won on a wing and a prayer, his follow-up title at Royal Birkdale in 2008 was a consummate display of controlled mastery. What made it even more astonishing was that a week before tee-off his participation was in severe doubt owing to a wrist injury; Harrington could barely practise.

High winds gusting off the Irish Sea made the task even trickier, and few had the Irishman down as favourite. Even fewer had Greg Norman, but the Great White Shark was rolling back the years, enjoying his golf in the company of his new wife Chris Evert (at least for a while). For the first three days, only Norman,

Dubliner Pádraig Harrington recovered from a wrist injury to overhaul Greg Norman, his playing partner in the final group, and record a magnificent back-to-back victory, becoming the first European to successfully defend the Open since James Braid in 1906.

Harrington and K. J. Choi seemed capable of doing battle with the elements. No one was under par.

The Korean's game collapsed on the final day, and a 77 did for Norman, who soon ceded victory to the Irishman. Harrington, regardless, shot 32 on the back nine and was able to walk up the 18th, beaming. Few golfers reach that comfort zone. His achievement in winning back-to-back Opens – and a PGA Championship too in 2008 – puts him up there with the modern greats.

Adlington: The Pride of Mansfield

THE SIGN on the bus read: 'Rebecca Adlington is the pride of Mansfield'. She was all that and more. The pride of the whole of Britain. Ten days before the wonderfully emotional open-top bus parade through her hometown, Adlington had swum the race of her life against the clock, the world-record clock, in the 800 metres freestyle.

Having left the other finalists floundering in her wake, she smashed the 19-year-old record, the longest standing in the sport, by an incredible 2.12 seconds. And only five days previously she had swum another race of her life in the 400 metres freestyle to win Britain's first female swimming Olympic gold for 48 years. With 10 metres to go, Katie Hoff of the USA had gold within her reach, half a length clear, with Adlington seemingly battling for silver with teammate Jo Jackson.

In the process of taking her penultimate stroke, Adlington glanced to her left to see she was level with the American. A split second later she touched home seven hundredths of a second ahead – the difference between the Briton's outstretched fingers and Hoff's flat palm – Jackson took bronze. 'A masterful swim' extolled the BBC commentator at the end of the 400 metres. After the second gold, the message was even clearer. 'Rebecca Adlington, you are absolutely brilliant.' Spot on.

Rebecca Adlington celebrates the race of her life after winning the 800 metres freestyle Olympic gold in a new world-record time of 8 minutes 17.51 seconds.

The Lightning Bolt

Bolt ran the perfect race, with flawless technique.

THERE IS something undeniably cool about being 'the fastest man on the planet'. The 100 metres world record has always had that special allure; that complete, undisputed No. 1 status. Breaking the 100 metres world record is always a global news event. And doing it at the Olympics, well, that really is something.

But it was the way that Usain Bolt obliterated the field in Beijing in 2008 that made his victory so breathtaking. Even without reigning world champion Tyson Gay in the final, Bolt's Jamaican teammate Asafa Powell was there, and, astonishingly, six men had run under ten seconds in the semi-finals. But that competition had disintegrated by halfway through the race. The 100 metres is meant to be a close contest, but it wasn't this time.

Three races, three golds and three world records: Usain Bolt held the world in thrall for eight glorious days during the Beijing Olympics.

Bolt was far ahead, and knew it. His chest-slapping celebrations as he slowed down way before the line may have attracted high-profile criticism afterwards, but it was the ultimate expression of 'I'm the man!' And how good must that have felt? Bolt was just after the gold medal, not the world record. But 9.72 had become 9.69, and he would soon break it again.

'Lightning never strikes twice?' – it's so obviously not true. And when you have a name as handy for the headline writers as Usain Bolt, it makes their job easy. The Lightning Bolt striking twice in Beijing in the 2008 Olympics was perhaps inevitable after his world record

-breaking performance in the 100 metres. The 200 metres – Bolt's preferred event, after all – provided even more of a juddering shock.

Even Michael Johnson thought that Bolt could not beat his world record of 19.32 set in Atlanta 12 years previously, and the Jamaican's cause was not helped by a headwind on the night of the final. But Bolt ran the perfect race, with flawless technique. And this time Bolt ran all out for the record as well as the gold medal, dipping on the line with just a quick glance at the clock – 19.30.

The world stopped and gawped while Bolt took his time, taking in the occasion and the achievement before striking his pose, removing his golden shoes and performing his dance. Lightning would strike a third time in the sprint relay. Another gold, for Jamaica. Another world record.

He took the opportunity to celebrate with a series of elaborate gestures that have made him one of the most famous athletes on the planet.

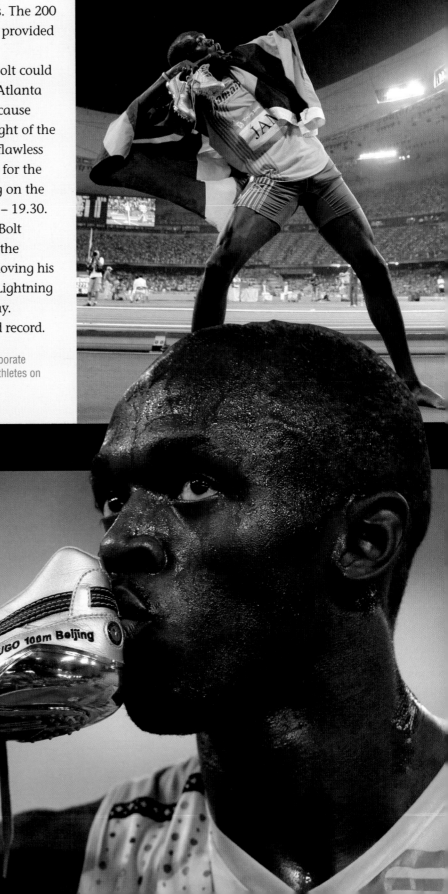

Hoy Scores a Hat-Trick

At the grand old age of 32, cyclist Chris Hoy was unstoppable in Beijing. Gold in the team sprint, gold in the keirin and gold in the individual sprint (above) earned him a golden hat-trick.

BRITAIN HAS always had an affinity with the bicycle, from the penny-farthing onwards, but never before have we dominated the sport so totally as at the Beijing Olympics. The roll call was just astonishing: 14 medals in total, eight of them gold, three for (soon to be Sir) Chris Hoy. With the more than honourable exception of Nicole Cooke – winner of a spectacular road race around the Great Wall for Britain's first gold of the Games – the track was where it was all happening.

Three pursuit races, three golds: Bradley Wiggins supreme, Rebecca Romero amazingly going one better than her rowing silver from Athens 2004. Three sprint races, three golds: Vicky Pendleton unbeatable in the women's race, Hoy a giant among men, this sprint title the crowning glory of his golden hat-trick. World records were shattered in the team races. The rest of the world were reduced to scraps – Australia a miserly silver, the USA one gold only, great cycling nations France and Spain two apiece.

It was Hoy, the great Scot, inevitably now the Flying Scotsman, who became the enduring symbol of Britain's most successful Olympics in a century. Immaculately prepared and motivated, the sport of cycling showed the way forward to true excellence, and as never before captured the public imagination. It was some ride.

Hull Give it Everything

THE 2008 Challenge Cup final was simply one of those great Wembley occasions. The sun was belting it down on to the greenest of pitches. The fans, from all over the land, were in the best of spirits. Quite apart from 'Abide With Me', the minute's silence in memory of rugby league legend Don Fox (see page 52), who had died the previous week, set an emotional scene.

St Helens were massive favourites, a supreme rugby league team at the height of its powers, but Hull, roared on by a sea of black and white clad fans, had done it before, in 2005 against Leeds, and they would give it absolutely everything. Predictably, Saints were ten points clear at half-time, but it could have been so many more were it not for the hardy Hull defence. Half-back Richard Horne, in his first game since injuring his neck in April, was taking a battering. But then … an interception, a Kirk Yeaman try. Then after another controversial call against St Helens, Yeaman again. Unbelievable. But it wasn't to be – the superior class of Leon Pryce, Sean Long, Kieron Cunningham and Paul Wellens soon told, and the final score read 28-16 – but as an advert for the game of rugby league, it was unbeatable.

Hull's Graeme Horne (brother of teammate Richard) tackles James Roby during a match in which clear favourites St Helens withstood a heroic second half comeback by the underdogs to claim their third consecutive Challenge Cup victory.

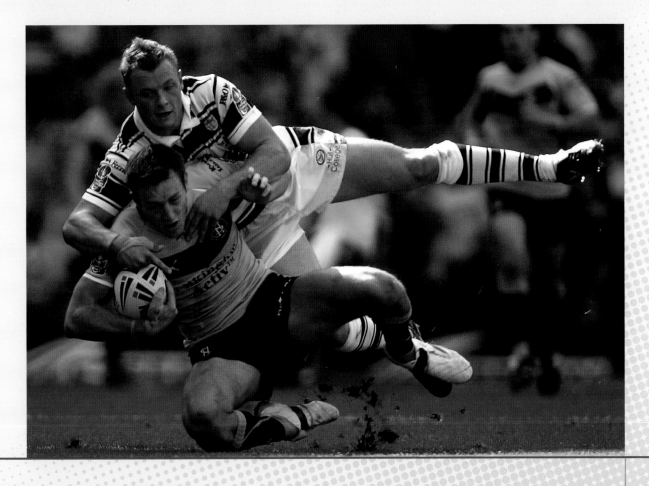

Walcott Crushes Croatia

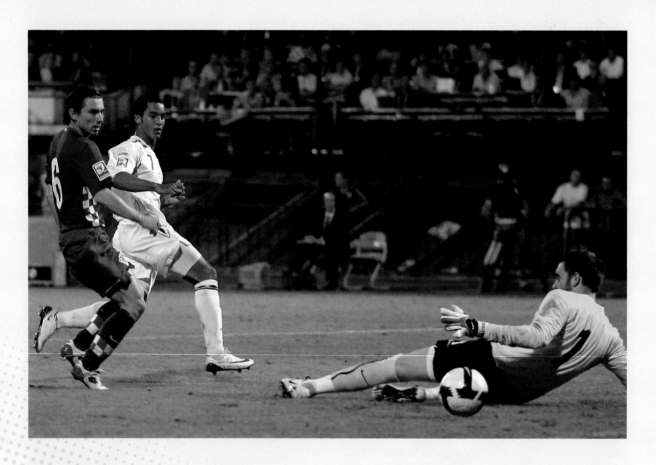

England's current nemesis, Croatia, were finally put to the sword when 19-year-old Arsenal striker Theo Walcott scored three times in a 4-1 win in Zagreb.

DRAWS HAVE a habit of seeming preordained, so there was an audible groan when England were paired with Croatia in their qualification group for the 2010 World Cup. Just four days had passed since defeat in the pouring rain at Wembley had ended both England's Euro 2008 hopes and the tenure of Steve McClaren, the 'Wally with the Brolly'. By the time Fabio Capello took England to Zagreb for the seemingly crucial qualifier, there were some grounds for optimism: a new man at the helm, a win in Andorra under their belts.

What happened that night was beyond anyone's expectations. The 19-year-old Theo Walcott, again starting ahead of David Beckham, simply terrorised the opposition defence with his speed, winning drive and pure instinct. A shot drilled into the corner put England in the lead midway through the first half, then after an hour, Walcott repeated the trick from Wayne Rooney's pass. Rooney got in on the act himself before setting Theo up to become the youngest player to score a hat-trick for England – 4-1 away! It was hard to fathom we were watching the same team that had lost so dismally at home against the same opponents. And temporarily at least, it exorcised so many demons.

A Good Experience

FOR ELEANOR Simmonds, the 2008 Paralympics were meant to be good experience. The real goal was London in four years' time. But like all sensible 13-year-olds, Ellie wasn't listening to her elders. In the Beijing Water Cube she just went out there to do her own thing. In considerable style.

With 25 metres to go in the S6 100 metres freestyle, she was in fourth, trailing the Dutch favourite Mirjam de Koning by some distance. But in her own words, Ellie kept her head down and went for it, touching home in first place, to become the youngest ever British gold medal winner. Her tears as she realised what she had achieved showed exactly what it meant to the Walsall schoolgirl. Days later, she repeated her gold medal-winning performance in the S6 400 metres freestyle, the event in which she held the world record.

Simmonds' remarkable exploits in the pool captured the imagination of the British public, and were formally recognised when she became the country's youngest recipient of an MBE in the New Year's Honours List in 2009. Summing up her Beijing experience, Simmonds described it as: 'Amazing. The best thing in the world.' Good experience, then. Hopefully London 2012 will top it for her.

The youngest athlete to compete at the 2008 Paralympics, aged 13, Eleanor stunned spectators when she won double gold in the S6 100 and 400 metres freestyle events. She went on to win ten World Championship golds in 2009 and 2010 and five European golds in 2009.

It's Hamilton – by a Whisker

FOR A while, we really thought he had blown it. Again. It was so cruel in 2007, with Lewis Hamilton losing the World Championship by a point to Kimi Räikkönen. Now here we were at Interlagos again. This time Hamilton only needed fifth place to clinch the title, but in the chaos of a Formula One race, anything could happen.

Rain was forecast. And much as he liked driving in the wet, Hamilton's aggressive approach had already blown one golden chance, at the Japanese Grand Prix. Now, from fourth on the grid, all Hamilton had to do was keep his McLaren out of trouble. Pit-stop strategy made the race unbearably tense: Timo Glock went ahead on dry tyres, then, as the drizzle began, Sebastian Vettel passed Hamilton with

Lewis Hamilton's Formula One championship in 2008 went right to the wire – the British driver snatched back the crown on the last corner in one of the most dramatic title deciders in history. A Hollywood script could not have been more exciting.

two laps to go, dropping the Englishman down to sixth place. Felipe Massa took the flag: Ferrari celebrated, thinking he was champion, in front of his own fans. Brazil was going nuts. Lewis just had to get ahead of Glock. And on the final corner, on the final lap, of the final race, the German could not hold it and the McLaren sailed past for fifth. Hamilton was champion. The scenes with his father Anthony and brother Nicholas were as emotional as it gets. Britain breathed a huge sigh of relief for (at that time) the youngest Formula One world champion.

BOXING *World Light Heavyweight Championship*
Joe Calzaghe v. Roy Jones Jr, Madison Square Garden, New York, 8 November 2008

2008

Part Seven 2000–2011

The Italian Dragon Bows Out in Style

UNDEFEATED. IT'S not a bad way to end your career, especially in a sport as brutal as boxing. And to win your final fight by a unanimous decision, at Madison Square Garden, against the great Roy Jones Jr – that's bowing out in some style.

Joe Calzaghe was vulnerable, that much was certain. Against Bernard Hopkins in Las Vegas in April, the Welshman's first ever fight in the States, he found himself on the canvas in the first round, but recovered to take the bout by a split decision. He was super-middleweight and now light-heavyweight champion of the world. WBO, IBF, WBA, WBC – you name it, Joe had won it. But Jones was Jones, pound for pound for years the absolute best, and a swollen wrist had hampered Calzaghe's preparations.

Anticipation for the fight was beyond feverish – Battle of the Superpowers, they called it. When they finally got it on, Calzaghe was put down again in the first round. Bleeding, the Italian Dragon came roaring back, finding his range with a barrage of blows, and even by the fourth round you knew Jones was a beaten man. All three judges scored it 118-109. Calzaghe threw 985 punches to 475 from the American. And after 46 fights, Calzaghe could retire. Undefeated. Champion of the world.

Just one of Calzaghe's 985 punches lands on the face of the challenger Roy Jones Jr as the Welshman's non-stop barrage resulted in a unanimous points victory.

Ireland's Grand Slam Party

Ronan O'Gara's drop-goal is on its way – advantage Ireland. Moments later the Welsh win a penalty. It looks good … but falls short and Ireland can start to party.

TO SAY Ireland's sensational 2009 Grand Slam victory came down to two kicks is to unfairly dismiss the ferocious intensity of the previous 398 minutes of the campaign, and in particular the 78 minutes that preceded the first of those kicks.

On the final weekend of the Six Nations, Wales went in 6-0 up at half-time against the Irish, but the visitors were made of tough stuff. Once Ronan O'Gara found his kicking boots, they turned on the style, with Brian O'Driscoll and Paul O'Connell in devastating form. But Welsh fervour was undiminished and with five minutes remaining, Stephen Jones landed a drop-goal to shatter Irish hopes. It was 15-14 to Wales. And so it really did come down to two kicks, but that wasn't one of them.

Two minutes to go, the Irish pack drives deep into Welsh territory. O'Gara lurks, the ball is fed to him, the Welsh defence charges but to no avail. Soaring sweetly over despairing hands, the drop-goal flies between the posts. Nailed it.

Seconds remaining. Irish fans are celebrating, until the harsh blast of a whistle cuts across them. Welsh penalty. From 48 metres, Jones is confident. He prepares to kick, the clock ticks to 80 minutes. He strikes the ball, straight. Behind the goal, it looks good, it is coming, it is going to make it, yes … no, just short, it fades away. Ireland's first Grand Slam in 61 years had been won in the most dramatic fashion. The party could begin in earnest.

Bloodgate

RUGBY HAS always held an advantage over football in that it is deemed to be fair – a ruffians' game played by gentlemen. OK, so there's a lot going on in scrums, rucks and mauls that you don't want to know about, but there's none of that namby-pamby stuff, diving (sorry, I mean simulation), feigning injury, that sort of thing.

Oh dear. Harlequins didn't just bring the game into disrepute in April 2009; they drove it kicking and screaming on to the front pages, then into the courts of law. It was pretty much as disgraceful as you could imagine, and it was hard to believe that someone like Dean Richards could be involved in it.

The former Leicester and England stalwart was as old-fashioned as rugby players got, surely? A real pints-down-the-hatch-after-the-game, everything-forgotten kind of bloke. A former policeman, let's not forget. Yet for some reason he had deemed it

Harlequins' Mike Brown launches a full-blooded tackle on Leinster's Rob Kearney, but the 'real' blood turned out to be fake as Quins' gamesmanship took a turn for the worst.

suitable for Quins physio Steph Brennan to issue fake blood capsules to the players, and for club doctor Wendy Chapman to make it look even more realistic with the quick swish of a blade.

But this time, wing Tom Williams was caught, despite Chapman cutting his lip to mask the fake blood (and his 'blood injury' replacement Nick Evans failed to score anyway – so much for that tactical substitution!). Leinster won the tight contest at The Stoop, 6-5, and went on to lift their first Heineken Cup. 'Bloodgate' the papers called it. It turned out they'd done it before. Fines and bans were handed out; the rugby authorities were seen to be doing the right thing. But will their sport ever be the same again?

TENNIS All England Lawn Tennis Championships
Men's Singles Semi-Final, Andy Murray v. Andy Roddick, Wimbledon, London, 2 July 2009

2009

Murray Chokes, Roddick Strikes

GOING INTO the 2009 Wimbledon semi-final, Andy Murray held a 6-2 head-to-head lead over Andy Roddick, having only dropped one set in the tournament. Roddick meanwhile had faced a brutal five-set quarter-final against Lleyton Hewitt. This was surely the moment for the Scot to break Britain's 71-year wait for a men's finalist.

From the outset the American was clearly not going to adopt his customary blood and guts approach, which might have allowed Murray to fire his deadly arrows down the line. Instead, Roddick held back and let his serve do the work. The key moment in the first set came at 30-30 in the tenth game, when even Murray could not reach Roddick's deft drop-shot. The break point was converted and the set duly sewn up. When Roddick tried the same trick in the first game of

Although he is undoubtedly one of the world's finest players, Andy Murray has so far been unable to win a Grand Slam. The match against Roddick was classic Murray; a huge effort, that was just not quite enough.

the second set, Murray was wise to it, on his way to a break and the set.

At 5-2, the third looked to be going the way of the American but Murray dug deep, producing fabulous tennis to force a tie-break and earn himself a set point, saved by a fortuitous volley. In that moment the match was perhaps lost. The fourth also went to a tie-break, and although Murray saved a match point with a wonderful cross-court backhand, it wasn't enough. Roddick went on to a classic encounter with Federer and Murray had to wait another year ... for another semi-final defeat.

Watson's Dream Almost Comes True

BOO. HISS. Poor Stewart Cink. Through no fault of his own, Cink became the pantomime villain who won the Open. The 138th Championship had all the elements of a fairy tale, but unfortunately for Tom Watson it was more Brothers Grimm than Hans Christian Andersen.

Thirty-two years after winning the 'Duel in the Sun' (see page 82) with Jack Nicklaus on the same Turnberry course, Watson was leading by a stroke going into the final round. Now 59 and sporting a replacement hip, age seemed to catch up with him as he dropped two early strokes. But following Kipling's advice, he kept his head while all about him were losing theirs.

First new leader Ross Fisher carded a horror eight on the fifth, then Lee Westwood dropped three shots in the final four holes. Standing on the 18th tee, Watson required only a par to beat clubhouse leader Cink and secure one of the most extraordinary sporting achievements ever.

A good drive left him an 8 or 9-iron to the green. He chose the 8, hit it sweetly and saw it pitch and run through to the fringe. A strong return putt sped 10 feet past the pin. This was it – one last stroke for glory. Watson sent the putt on its way but it was never true, drifting short and right. The resultant playoff was all Cink but the standing ovations were Watson's. As he said afterwards, with a rueful smile, 'It was almost, almost. The dream almost came true.'

Phlegmatic in his defeat, the always wise Tom Watson said, 'Honestly, it's not the most important thing in life. I've always lived life out on tour where, after a disappointment, it's onward to the next week … Forget what happened in the past, except where it might help you to play better golf.'

Freddie Strikes Again

ON THE eve of the Second Ashes Test between England and Australia at Lord's in 2009, Andrew Flintoff announced his retirement from Test cricket. After the battering he had given his body over the years, this would be his last series. The stage was set for a grand performance.

England had scraped a draw with a last-wicket stand in the First Test in Cardiff, and the Ashes were there to be reclaimed. At first, Flintoff disappointed. Just four runs in the first innings, as Andrew Strauss and Alastair Cook gave England a perfect start. Only one wicket when Australia batted, even if it was the big one of Mike Hussey. The Aussies were then set over 500 to win, surely an impossible task,

especially when Flintoff dismissed both openers. Unbelievably though, they were still in it on the final morning. And then came Freddie.

A devastating burst of hostile bowling accounted for Brad Haddin, caught by Paul Collingwood, and then Nathan Hauritz and Peter Siddle were powerless, clean bowled, annihilated. Flintoff struck the pose and took the plaudits for his first ever, only ever, five-wicket haul at the home of cricket. His name was on the Honours Board for eternity. The Ashes would be won; Freddie's final bow would never be forgotten.

Fast, aggressive and effective just when he needed to be – Flintoff unleashes yet another thunderbolt, that gives Australia's Mike Hussey little time to take evasive action as the ball flashes past his helmet.

Mark Cavendish Leads the Way

Out on his own: Cav wins the 21st and final stage of the Tour de France, the highlight of a tremendous year for the Manx Missile.

IN 2009 Mark Cavendish announced to the world of cycling that he was the fastest man on two wheels. The Manx Missile had already won four stages of the 2008 Tour de France – unprecedented for a British rider – to go with a gold medal with Bradley Wiggins in the Madison at the World Championships and two stage wins in the Giro d'Italia. When the 2009 Tour came around, he seemed unstoppable.

Set up for his sprint finishes by the clockwork efficiency and blistering speed of the HTC-Columbia team train, Cavendish won the second, third, tenth and eleventh stages, becoming in the process the first Briton to wear the green jersey for two days in a row. Victory in Stage 19 took him past Barry Hoban's record of nine Tour de France stage wins, and one more on

the cobblestones of the Champs-Élysées in Stage 21, ahead of his lead-out man Mark Renshaw, proved beyond any doubt that he was the man to beat. Britain was leading the world in cycling, and Cav was out in front.

Phillips Idowu Walks the Walk

WHEN YOU talk the talk, it's rather important that you can walk the walk. We like our eccentrics in sport, but also prefer that they're not all dressed up with nowhere to go. So for Phillips Idowu – with his day-glo hair and piercings and general largeness of attitude – imagine how good it felt to get that gold medal round his neck.

So long the nearly man, the 'unexploded bomb' as *The Times* once called him, and of course always in the shadow of Jonathan Edwards, Idowu again had his work cut out going into the World Championships in Berlin. The heartbreak of Beijing the previous year was still raw; Idowu the favourite, nudged down to silver. And, of course, there was also Nelson Evora of Portugal, reigning world and Olympic

Born and bred in Hackney – mean streets that he once thought he could never leave – it seems ironic that Phillips Idowu is heading back there for the 2012 Olympics with a chance to win more gold.

champion. The Cubans would be in the reckoning too, as ever. But mostly Evora, who had leapt a season's best three months earlier in Brazil.

This time, though, the Londoner got it all right on the night. The triple jump is all about timing. Evora went out to 17.54 metres; Idowu 3 centimetres behind. But then in the third round, Idowu responded with a personal best, 17.73, and Evora this time was unable to respond. Cue the largest grin in Berlin. A European gold and another PB would follow in 2010. Roll on London in 2012.

Bolt Goes Ballistic

USAIN BOLT'S world record-breaking performances at the Beijing Olympics in 2008 had left us in no doubt as to who was the fastest man in the world. He was always going to be the star of the World Athletics Championships in Berlin in 2009 (even if the ubiquitous mascot Berlino the bear tried to usurp his position).

What we did not know was just how much of a star Bolt would become. To judge by the Jamaican's expression at the end of the 100 metres final, even he did not know. The scoreboard read 9.58! More than a tenth of a second off the previous record! That just didn't happen – had never happened since the advent of electronic timing. Bolt's greatest rival in the race, Tyson Gay of the USA, ran 9.71 yet was blitzed once again.

Just before he stepped into the blocks for the 100 metres, Usain Bolt made a single swoop of the arm, mimicking a bird or a plane … or even Superman. Just how much faster can he go?

Bolt seemed to run round the whole track while slowing down. It was less a lap of honour than a space shuttle landing. The crowd went ballistic. Then, in the 200 metres – with both finals uncannily a year to the day since Beijing – there was another monstrous milestone: 19.19. There was a prosaic explanation for both records – Bolt had improved his reaction time at the gun – but this was as jaw dropping as sport gets. It was simply unbelievable.

Sea The Stars Takes His Place at the Top Table

THE GREATEST racehorse of all time? The greatest in living memory? Jockey Mick Kinane called him the horse of a lifetime. The debate over where Sea The Stars sits in the pantheon of racing gods will be enjoyed for an age. The only thing certain is that following his immaculate three-year-old season in 2009, he is worthy of a place at the top table alongside Ribot, Sea Bird II, Secretariat, Dancing Brave, Mill Reef and Brigadier Gerard, among others.

It seems barely believable now, but when Sea The Stars began his stratospheric 2009 Group One campaign, no one was entirely sure of the extent of his ability. But that didn't last long. The 2,000 Guineas demonstrated his devastating pace. Stamina? Proven in his Epsom Derby victory. Intelligence? He knew how to win by just enough, as he showed in defeating Rip van Winkle in the Eclipse. Strength and consistency? A hard season racing and training was all but rounded off with two further Group One victories in the Juddmonte International Stakes at York and the Irish Champion Stakes at Leopardstown.

On 4 October all these attributes came together in his final race when Sea The Stars emulated his mother by winning the Prix de l'Arc de Triomphe with a display of style and never-before-seen acceleration. He became the first ever horse to win this, the 2,000 Guineas and the Derby in the same year. Credentials? Perhaps second to none.

Sea The Stars is ridden to victory by 50-year-old jockey Mick Kinane in the Irish Champion Stakes at Leopardstown in Dublin.

Tweddle Bounces Back

WHO WOULD have thought that Britain would become good at gymnastics! Against all those dynamic Chinese, lithe Russians and screaming Americans, we didn't stand a chance, surely? Beth Tweddle turned all that around.

By far the best gymnast the country has ever produced, the girl from Liverpool had been rewarded with her fair share of medals over the years, including a World Championships gold in her favourite event, the uneven bars, in 2006, but her crowning glory came on home soil – or rather mat – in 2009. This World Championships had not gone well for Tweddle, now 24 and a positive veteran in the sport. After falling from the uneven bars, she failed to qualify for the final. Disaster and a crushing disappointment for the London crowd. Qualification in the floor went better, but only just. Where was her rhythm? It was time to pull out all the stops in the final on Sunday, and how she did.

Choosing a routine with a level of difficulty way above her competitors, it could have gone one of two ways. Tweddle was breathtakingly brilliant. From tumbles and twists to majestic control of the space, she enraptured the O2 Arena and a nation watching at home. Britain! Gold in gymnastics! Who'd have thought it?

Gymnastics is another sport that Britain shouldn't really be good at, but Beth Tweddle is a three-time world champion, and widely considered to be the most successful British gymnast of all time.

Button Sews it Up

IN MARCH 2009 the phoenix rose from the ashes once again, this time in the guise of a Formula One team, Brawn GP. Born only two weeks before the 2009 F1 season, out of the demise of Honda Racing, the mythical bird soared above the Grand Prix paddocks of the world, with Jenson Button and Rubens Barrichello along for the ride.

In its inaugural race in Australia, Brawn recorded a one-two finish, with Button on top. The season then seemed to be a triumphant procession towards the title for the 29-year-old Briton, with five wins in the following six races, China the only blemish on a perfect scorecard. Then came the chilly British Grand Prix at Silverstone, when the wheels appeared to come off Button's year, or rather the heat disappeared from his tyres as he slumped to a sixth-placed finish.

Jenson Button started the season like a train, with six wins in seven races, then tightened up as he succumbed to the pressure of leading the championship. But he held on to win the drivers' title for the first time in his ten-year career.

Only one podium position followed in the next seven races as Button's challengers swapped victories, but failed to put together a concerted surge. By the penultimate race of the season in Brazil, he led his teammate Barrichello by 14 points, with Sebastian Vettel two points further back. Starting from a disappointing 14th on the grid, Button battled to fifth, securing the necessary points for a well-deserved championship victory. After Lewis Hamilton in 2008, it was Britain's first consecutive drivers' title since Graham Hill and Jackie Stewart in 1962 and 1963. Button's playboy image was at last consigned to the scrapheap. Well, partly.

The Hayemaker Slays the Monster

'HEAVYWEIGHT CHAMPION of the world'. There's no bigger title in boxing. But when David Haye took on Nikolai Valuev for the WBA World Championship belt in November 2009, there was an even bigger dimension – Valuev himself.

Fighters come in all shapes and sizes but the Russian was just ridiculous – 7-foot 2-inches tall with a face only a mother could love, the man is simply huge. The Hayemaker, up at this level from cruiserweight, looked tiny in comparison. Yet in true David v. Goliath fashion (as the fight was billed), size just did not matter. Even with Valuev effectively on home ground, the Londoner proved once again that there's no substitute for boxing skills.

Jabbing, ducking and diving when necessary, consistently finding his range, it was a sensational performance by the Bermondsey boy. In a blistering final round (and with a broken hand), it even seemed as though Haye would put Valuev on the canvas for the first time in his career. Even with the vagaries of the judging system, there was only one winner. Haye became Britain's first heavyweight world champion since Lennox Lewis. And he defeated an ogre to do it.

A minute-looking David Haye aims a shot at Valuev's midriff – how he intended to get at the Russian's head and face is anyone's guess. Nonetheless, he did it and took the WBA world heavyweight crown for his efforts.

Robert Green's Gaffe

IF IT had happened during a Premier League match between West Ham and Fulham, you could almost have laughed it off. These things happen, after all. But on the first Saturday night of the World Cup, England a hotbed of anticipation before their first match against the USA, the toughest opponents in Group C ... poor old Robert Green.

The keeper's spilling of Clint Dempsey's speculative shot just before half-time in Rustenburg set the tone for an abject tournament, one that had started so brightly with England skipper Steven Gerrard's opener just four minutes into the match. Six months build-up – all for this. Some people blamed the Jabulani ball, but it was really just an error brought on by nerves (as well as faulty technique?), and for that Fabio Capello can take his share of the blame.

Far from being the confident architect of winning teams, the England manager became an isolated figure as well as an indecisive leader who went back on his earlier promises, and that seam of uncertainty – from his wavering choice of No. 1 to other mystifying selections and substitutions – fatally undermined England's chances. We thought this time it would be different. Someone had to be the fall guy. Green will never live this down.

These things always seem to happen in slow motion – and this was no exception. Robert Green claws the air in a frantic attempt to stop the ball crossing the line. It was the shape of things to come in a dreadful tournament for England.

G-Mac Ends 40 Years of Hurt

PRIOR TO 2010, anyone throwing a party to celebrate the last European winner of the US Open would most likely have been dancing to the big No. 1 of the day, 'In the Summertime' by Mungo Jerry. In local cinemas Ryan O'Neal and Ali MacGraw starred in a classic weepie, but Tony Jacklin's victory in 1970 did not mark the start of a European *Love Story*. A better choice would have been Burt Lancaster in *Airport*, because the next 40 years proved to be a disaster for our golfers.

All that changed with Graeme McDowell. Going into the final round three shots behind Dustin Johnson, he watched the American implode by the fourth hole. Forced to play his third shot at the second left-handed in order to find a stance, Johnson carded a triple bogey, followed by a double and a single. Game over. Phil Mickelson looked to be making a charge when he birdied the first, but that proved his only move of the round. Ernie Els briefly joined McDowell in the lead but he and Tiger Woods spent too much time near beaches or cliffs to exert much pressure. Eventually the only challenge came from the unheralded Frenchman Grégory Havret, who had a putt on the 18th to tie the lead. He missed and McDowell had two putts for his first Major.

At the celebratory party in his hometown of Portrush, Northern Ireland, who knows whether they were singing along to the No. 1 of the day? It was 'Shout for England' by Dizzee Rascal and James Corden.

'Winning Majors is not about talent, it is about hearts and minds,' Tony Jacklin, the last European winner of the US Open, said before this year's tournament. In 2010, Graeme McDowell showed he had all the necessary qualities.

Mo Farah's Double European Gold

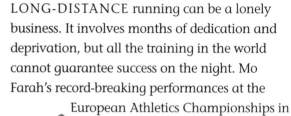

LONG-DISTANCE running can be a lonely business. It involves months of dedication and deprivation, but all the training in the world cannot guarantee success on the night. Mo Farah's record-breaking performances at the European Athletics Championships in Barcelona in the summer of 2010 were a personal triumph and completed a haul of six gold medals for Great Britain.

Farah had already set the ball rolling by becoming the first Briton to win the 10,000 metres, ahead of compatriot Chris Thompson in a superb second place, before the pair lined up again five days later to contest the 5,000 metres. The energy-sapping nature of competing in both races means that double golds are rare in these events, and had never before been achieved by a British athlete, not even the great Brendan Foster.

The home crowd got behind defending champion Jesus Espana, but, just as in the 10,000 metres, Farah toyed with the other runners and then broke them in a mesmerising display of tactical running. It capped an astonishing comeback for the Somali-born Londoner, who had collapsed after two races earlier in the season, and was met with a scream of joy, then tears. Sometimes the hard work does pay off.

Mo Farah upgraded his 5,000 metres silver medal from 2006 to claim Great Britain's first ever 10,000 metres gold in European Athletics Championship history in Barcelona before repeating the feat in the 5,000 metres.

England Go Out on Penalties ... Again!

ON PAPER, it was a one-sided World Cup semi-final. The previous best England's women had managed was fourth in 1990. In 2006 they came seventh. From five group games, they won three, drew one and lost one, scoring seven goals. The Netherlands, on the other hand, were reigning world, Olympic and European champions, played five, won five, scoring 25 goals. In their previous six World Cup encounters, the Dutch had won all six. But with the sensational Beth Storry in goal, there was always a chance.

The Dutch had the better of the first half chances, but Storry and the English defence held firm. In the 56th minute their perseverance was rewarded when Hannah Macleod dived in to tuck away a superb Crista Cullen cross. The Dutch were not champions for nothing, however, taking the match to extra time with a 61st-minute penalty corner. Eventually it was down to the curse of English sport – penalties. At 2-2 skipper Kate Walsh stepped up, put it to her left, just in reach of the Dutch goalkeeper's glove. Charlotte Craddock followed, but a nervy flick was easily turned away. Storry had to save the last two. She managed the first but couldn't stop the second. A tearful England were not heading to the final, but the smiles returned with a 2-0 victory over Germany to secure a best ever third place. Don't write them off for London 2012.

England captain Kate Walsh is consoled by teammates after England's 5-4 defeat to the Netherlands in the World Cup semi-final.

Chris Ashton Raises the Roof

UNTIL ONE autumn day not so very long ago, the jury was still out on Martin Johnson's England. A new generation of players had finally been promoted into the starting line-up, but did they really have what it takes, especially against the southern hemisphere sides?

We found out when Australia were torn apart by some of the most devastating attacking rugby seen at Headquarters in years. Ben Youngs was at the heart of most of it and was a deserving man-of-the-match. Toby Flood's place kicking completely outshone his counterpart James O'Connor and his 25 points was a record for an Englishman against Australia. Mark Cueto deserved a try, while Chris Ashton lifted the Twickenham roof.

Chris Ashton received the ball in his own 22 and accelerated to the halfway line. Drew Mitchell came across to cut him out, but the Northampton wing showed deft footwork as well as pace to leave him on the floor and stretch England's lead to 20 points. Pure class!

Ashton's second, game-killing score started on England's line as they repelled wave after wave of Wallabies attacks. Tom Palmer, another outstanding performer on the day, wrestled the ball back. Youngs broke, executed a neat sidestep, fed Courtney Lawes and then it was over to Ashton. The Northampton wing tore down the line. Drew Mitchell tried to cover. Not a chance. A change of direction, another blistering burst of speed. Exhilarating.

It finished 35-18 and the monkey was well and truly off England's backs. We hope they did not flatter to deceive.

England at the Top of the Tree

They must have been sick of the sight of him: Alistair Cook cuts another boundary as he grinds India into the ground on his way to 294, the most any batsman has ever scored in a Test innings at Edgbaston.

THE RENAISSANCE of the England Test cricket team began as far back as 1999 with the appointment of Zimbabwean Duncan Fletcher as coach. Improved performances, both home and away, culminated in the first Ashes series victory for 18 years in 2005. His new professional approach paved the way for his fellow countryman Andy Flower, who took the reins in 2009. Since then, ably led by skipper Andrew Strauss, series wins against the West Indies, Pakistan, Sri Lanka, Bangladesh and Australia – twice, including the Ashes again in Australia during the winter of 2010-11 had taken England to the brink of world domination.

Cue the arrival of India, the current No. 1 Test side. Underprepared and missing some key players, India were well beaten at both Lord's and Trent Bridge. Despite that, they were still not prepared for what happened in the Third Test at Edgbaston. Dismissed for 224 in their first innings they could only watch and admire as England racked up 710 for 7 declared – their third highest ever Test total – with Alistair Cook making a colossal 294 in a 13-hour innings. India were duly dispatched to defeat by an innings and 242 runs. The victory earned England enough points to secure the world's No. 1 Test team spot in the ICC World Rankings. The view from the top is ... fine thanks.

2011

Team GB Get the Job Done in Daegu

Commenee announced that he expected seven medals, including one gold.

THE HEAD coach of UK Athletics, Dutchman Charles van Commenee, is a hard man to please. When Kelly Sotherton won an Olympic bronze in the heptathlon in Athens in 2004, when he was heptathlon coach, he called her a 'wimp' for not winning the silver. Appointed to his new post in 2008, Commenee is renowned for setting stiff targets for the track and field team, in terms of preparation for and medals required from the major events. In Beijing in 2008, the team fell short, winning four medals instead of the expected five.

The World Championships in Daegu in 2011 offered the UK team a chance of redemption. Van Commenee announced that he expected seven medals, including one gold. His team took up the challenge. Mo Farah ran a thrilling 10,000 metres, but was caught 10 metres from the line

(Left) Dai Greene put in a powerful sprint to beat Puerto Rico's Javier Coulson to the line and take Britain's first gold of the games. The last came courtesy of the effervescent Mo Farah (above) in the 5,000 metres.

by Ethiopia's Ibrahim Jeilan and had to settle for silver. Lady Luck smiled on Andy Turner who was fortunate to be promoted to the bronze medal position in the 110 metres hurdles when the winner, Cuba's Dayron Robles, was disqualified. She did not smile for heptathlete and poster girl Jessica Ennis. Despite leading after four events, a poor performance in the javelin, her weakest discipline, meant she too had to settle for silver.

Day Six brought two medals. Hannah England surprised everyone, not least herself, to power down the home straight, overtake Spain's Natalia Rodriguez in the last few strides and take second

(Left) Hannah England was delighted with her silver in the 1,500 metres, but in complete contrast Jessica Ennis (below) was disappointed with a poor showing in the javelin, which meant she had to settle for silver in the heptathlon.

So, job done, and with one extra gold.

place in the 1,500 metres. Welshman Dai Greene went one better. He kept his cool after a false start in the 400 metres hurdles. Away second time, he was fourth over the penultimate hurdle but surged home to take Team GB's first gold medal of the championships.

The final day of competition brought more gold, as Mo Farah won the 5,000 metres from the front, running a race that former world record holder David Moorcroft hailed as 'perfection'. There might have been another gold for Phillips Idowu in the triple jump, but he was pushed into the silver medal position by an enormous last jump from the American Christian Taylor. So, job done, and with one extra gold. Of course, Commenee wants more from London 2012. It remains to be seen if his athletes can take up the challenge … again.